D0335283

POEMS ON
THE UNDERGROUND

POEMS
ON THE
UNDERGROUND

ANNIVERSARY EDITION

edited by
Gerard Benson
Judith Chernaik
Cicely Herbert

CASSELL

Cassell Publishers Limited
Wellington House, 125 Strand
London WC2R 0BB

100 Poems on the Underground
first published 1991
Poems on the Underground Illustrated Edition
first published 1992
Poems on the Underground New and Extended Edition
first published 1993
Poems on the Underground Fourth Edition
first published 1994
Poems on the Underground Fifth Edition
first published 1995
Poems on the Underground Anniversary Edition
first published 1996

British Library Cataloguing in Publication Data
A catalogue record for this book is available from the British Library

ISBN 0–304–34858–9

Typeset in Monotype Meridien by
KDI, Newton le Willows, Lancs.

Printed and bound in Great Britain by
Mackays of Chatham PLC, Chatham, Kent

CONTENTS

LIST OF ILLUSTRATIONS

LIST OF UNDERGROUND POSTERS

INTRODUCTION

Wʜᴇɴ Poems on the Underground was launched ten years ago, we hoped that London's two million commuters would be charmed to discover poems by Shelley and Burns, Seamus Heaney and Grace Nichols enlivening their daily Tube journeys. We little guessed that our dream of scattering poetry about in public places would be adopted by mass transport systems in New York, Paris, Dublin and Stuttgart, in capital cities in Scandinavia and Australia, and in scores of smaller cities in the UK and abroad. London's Poems on the Underground are now assumed to be part of the urban landscape, a model for primary school projects and a subject for Ph.D. theses in media studies and semiology.

The idea of poetry on public transport remains somewhat far-fetched, if not preposterous – and in this may lie its appeal. We have been credited in official Government surveys with inspiring a renewal of the art and appreciation of poetry; more people are writing poetry than ever before, more poetry titles are published, more poets performing in pubs and shopping malls, reciting alongside jazz bands and string quartets.

At the same time, for many people who care about litera-ture, poetry remains a private and somewhat obscure and esoteric passion. Perhaps this is one source of the popularity of our scheme, which is quiet and unobtrusive, a matter of a poem appearing here and there, at irregular intervals, in a space usually given over to seductive claims for car insurance or duty-free whisky.

Equally appealing, probably, is the fact that we have no hidden agenda, no allegiance to any particular school or move-ment. The choice of poems remains eclectic, as it has been from the start, dictated chiefly by the space available. We include at least two living poets in each group of five or six; for the remaining poems we draw on as wide and varied a list as possible, including light verse, in which English poetry excels, and the unsung 'Anon.' The common themes of poetry through the ages recur: love, death, time, memory, exile, the seasons, and a subject of inexhaustible interest to poets, the nature of the art itself, variously defined in our collection by Shakespeare, Keats and Dylan Thomas, Osip Mandelstam and Czeslaw Milosz, Elizabeth Bishop, Pablo Neruda and George Mackay Brown.

People often ask how we go about choosing the poems to be displayed on the Tube. It is hard to imagine a more purely pleasurable way of working than ours. The selection of each new group follows weeks of digging through our own libraries and the great public collections, from the medieval manuscripts in the British Library to the superb 20th-century holdings of the Poetry Library on the South Bank.

Once we have agreed on a set of poems, we try them out on a range of readers, young and old. We usually end up convincing ourselves that this particular set is the most accessible, most delightful in all possible ways. Often the public seems to agree; as they are posted on the Tube, poems often are reprinted in national and local newspapers and read on the radio. 'At Lord's' featured in the *Guardian* cricket diary; Andrew Salkey's 'A song for England' in the weather report, and Roger McGough's 'The Leader' in several political columns.

Not only do we become singularly attached to each new group of poems, we also become very fond of the posters. The printers' over-run of the first set led to a policy of printing twice as many posters as are actually displayed on the Tube, and over the years these have found their way into classrooms, hospitals, even prisons, many of which offer creative writing courses as an aid to therapy and rehabilitation. British Council libraries throughout the world subscribe to the posters, as do many schools and libraries in the UK. We often receive phone calls about poems identified by a single line or a striking metaphor ('the poem about the plums/bananas/the cat'; 'the one with the clock going backward'); usually the caller needs the poem immediately, to send to a friend or lover, to read at a school assembly, a wedding or funeral.

Inevitably, we retain a perverse affection for certain poems, especially from the earliest selections. Sir Thomas Wyatt's cryptic

'Tagus farewell' must have been extremely puzzling to many Tube travellers, but we still get enquiries about it. 'Trail all your pikes ... Ye silent, ye dejected men of war', by the 18th-century poet Anne Finch, Countess of Winchilsea, seemed risky, but was strangely apposite on the Tube at rush hour. Another special favourite, reprinted in a full page piece in London's *Evening Standard*, was 'I have a gentil cock', the bawdy 15th-century poem discovered in a manuscript in the British Library. Virtually each contemporary poet featured, serious or comic, well known or relatively obscure, has won a following which cuts across all ages and backgrounds.

One by-product of the programme has been a friendly corre-spondence with similar schemes abroad, leading to overlap-ping choices; Edwin Morgan's 'The Subway Piranhas', rejected in Glasgow, appeared on the Paris Metro in French translation. A year after our own launch, we were invited to Dublin for the launch of 'Poems on the Dart' – posters in green ink on the coastal railway, with station names evoking the ghosts of Yeats, Joyce and Beckett. In 1994 we exchanged poems with New York City's 'Poetry in Motion', run by the New York City Transit Authority; poems by Rita Dove and Thom Gunn dis-placed train announcements at Grand Central Station during the cheerful launch party. More recently, we have exchanged poems with Stockholm Transport (Kipling in Stockholm, Pär Lagerkvist, translated by Auden, in London); and last year, as part of the British Council 50th anniversary celebrations in Scandinavia, poems by Wendy Cope, James Berry, Sheenagh Pugh and Derek Mahon featured on Helsinki trams, with po-ems by Ted Hughes and Jean 'Binta' Breeze displayed in Oslo.

From the start, widespread public interest in the programme has led to a number of related activities: annual poetry readings at the British Library, as part of the Stefan Zweig series; poetry workshops at schools and libraries, and occasion-ally in more unlikely places, including, one chill September dawn, Westminster Bridge. The London Transport Museum has been the setting for readings and children's workshops, and on several occasions we were able to arrange displays of children's poems on the Underground.

The close links between poetry and song, seen in the earliest poems in our collection, 'Sumer is icumen in' and 'Western wind', have inspired several commissions in association with the Apollo Chamber Orchestra: new poems for a performance of Saint-Saëns' *Carnival of the Animals*; musical settings for love songs by W.H. Auden and Maya Angelou; a rock score for a reading of Christina Rossetti's *Goblin Market*, performed at the National Portrait Gallery and videoed for the British Library; and new arrangements of Sir John Betjeman's 'London Poems', with music by Jim Parker, and the 'Cries of London' by Orlando Gibbons. Last year, Wigmore Hall invited young composers to set to music a group of poems from our collection, later performed in workshop and concert; and the composer Thea Musgrave has set three groups of 'Poems on the Underground' for unaccompanied choir.

A fresh departure this past year was our first poetry competition, underwritten and co-judged by *The Times Literary Supplement*. An invitation to new and established poets for short poems on urban themes generated over 3,000 entries, many of an extremely high standard, with three prize-winning poems displayed on Underground trains in November, and included in this anthology.

We have been fortunate in securing the support both of London Transport and the London Arts Board, and we hope that we can continue as we began, in a spirit of guarded optimism about the future of public art, and boundless enthusiasm for the glories of English poetry. Although some fine and exciting poems do not lend themselves to display on the Underground (Blake's 'O Rose thou art sick' may have conveyed an alarming message to travellers in the bowels of the earth), there remains an apparently inexhaustible supply of delightful, funny, witty, astonishing and consoling poems that seem exactly right for the Underground. It is a privilege to be able to share them with the travelling public.

Gerard Benson, Judith Chernaik, Cicely Herbert
London, 1996

THE POEMS

Up in the Morning Early

Cauld blaws the wind frae east to west,
   The drift is driving sairly;
Sae loud and shrill's I hear the blast,
   I'm sure it's winter fairly.

CHORUS: Up in the morning's no for me,
   Up in the morning early;
When a' the hills are cover'd wi' snaw,
   I'm sure it's winter fairly.

The birds sit chittering in the thorn,
   A' day they fare but sparely;
And lang's the night frae e'en to morn,
   I'm sure it's winter fairly.

CHORUS: Up in the morning's no for me,
   Up in the morning early;
When a' the hills are cover'd wi' snaw,
   I'm sure it's winter fairly.

ROBERT BURNS (1759–96)

Ozymandias

I met a traveller from an antique land
Who said: Two vast and trunkless legs of stone
Stand in the desert . . . Near them, on the sand,
Half sunk, a shattered visage lies, whose frown,
And wrinkled lip, and sneer of cold command,
Tell that its sculptor well those passions read
Which yet survive, stamped on these lifeless things,
The hand that mocked them and the heart that fed;
And on the pedestal these words appear:
"My name is OZYMANDIAS, king of kings:
Look on my works, ye Mighty, and despair!"
Nothing beside remains. Round the decay
Of that colossal wreck, boundless and bare
The lone and level sands stretch far away.

PERCY BYSSHE SHELLEY (1792–1822)

This Is Just to Say

I have eaten
the plums
that were in
the icebox

and which
you were probably
saving
for breakfast

Forgive me
they were delicious
so sweet
and so cold

WILLIAM CARLOS WILLIAMS (1883–1963)

The Railway Children

When we climbed the slopes of the cutting
We were eye-level with the white cups
Of the telegraph poles and the sizzling wires.

Like lovely freehand they curved for miles
East and miles west beyond us, sagging
Under their burden of swallows.

We were small and thought we knew nothing
Worth knowing. We thought words travelled the wires
In the shiny pouches of raindrops,

Each one seeded full with the light
Of the sky, the gleam of the lines, and ourselves
So infinitesimally scaled

We could stream through the eye of a needle.

SEAMUS HEANEY (b. 1939)

Like a Beacon

In London
every now and then
I get this craving
for my mother's food
I leave art galleries
in search of plantains
saltfish/sweet potatoes

I need this link

I need this touch
of home
swinging my bag
like a beacon
against the cold

GRACE NICHOLS (b. 1950)

Sonnet 29

When in disgrace with Fortune and men's eyes,
I all alone beweep my outcast state,
And trouble deaf heaven with my bootless cries,
And look upon myself and curse my fate,
Wishing me like to one more rich in hope,
Featured like him, like him with friends possessed,
Desiring this man's art, and that man's scope,
With what I most enjoy contented least,
Yet in these thoughts myself almost despising,
Haply I think on thee, and then my state
(Like to the lark at break of day arising
From sullen earth) sings hymns at heaven's gate,
    For thy sweet love remembered such wealth brings,
    That then I scorn to change my state with kings.

WILLIAM SHAKESPEARE (1564–1616)

Her Anxiety

Earth in beauty dressed
Awaits returning spring.
All true love must die,
Alter at the best
Into some lesser thing.
Prove that I lie.

Such body lovers have,
Such exacting breath,
That they touch or sigh.
Every touch they give,
Love is nearer death.
Prove that I lie.

W. B. YEATS (1865–1939)

Lady 'Rogue' Singleton

Come, wed me, Lady Singleton,
And we will have a baby soon
And we will live in Edmonton
Where all the friendly people run.

I could never make you happy, darling,
Or give you the baby you want,
I would always very much rather, dear,
Live in a tent.

I am not a cold woman, Henry,
But I do not feel for you,
What I feel for the elephants and the miasmas
And the general view.

STEVIE SMITH (1902–71)

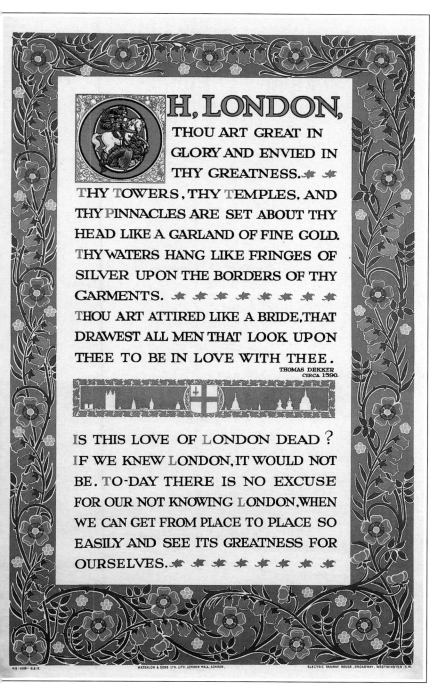

OH, LONDON, THOU ART GREAT IN GLORY AND ENVIED IN THY GREATNESS. THY TOWERS, THY TEMPLES, AND THY PINNACLES ARE SET ABOUT THY HEAD LIKE A GARLAND OF FINE GOLD. THY WATERS HANG LIKE FRINGES OF SILVER UPON THE BORDERS OF THY GARMENTS. THOU ART ATTIRED LIKE A BRIDE, THAT DRAWEST ALL MEN THAT LOOK UPON THEE TO BE IN LOVE WITH THEE.

THOMAS DEKKER
CIRCA 1590.

IS THIS LOVE OF LONDON DEAD? IF WE KNEW LONDON, IT WOULD NOT BE. TO-DAY THERE IS NO EXCUSE FOR OUR NOT KNOWING LONDON, WHEN WE CAN GET FROM PLACE TO PLACE SO EASILY AND SEE ITS GREATNESS FOR OURSELVES.

WATERLOW & SONS LTD. LITH. LONDON WALL, LONDON.   ELECTRIC RAILWAY HOUSE, BROADWAY, WESTMINSTER, S.W.

1 *Oh, London* **Charles Sharland** 1915

WHEN daisies go, shall winter time
Silver the simple grass with rime;
Autumnal frosts enchant the pool
And make the cart-ruts beautiful;
And when snowbright the moor expands,
How shall your children clap their hands!
To make this earth our hermitage
A cheerful and a changeful page,
God's bright and intricate device
Of days and seasons doth suffice.
          R. L. Stevenson in "Underwoods."

UNDERGROUND

THE WAY OF ESCAPE
TO THE COUNTRYSIDE

THE WESTMINSTER PRESS

2 *The Way of Escape to the Countryside* **Harry Becker** 1913

"FLEET upon fleet; argosy upon argosy. Masts to the right, masts to the left, masts in front, masts yonder above the warehouses; masts in among the streets as steeples appear amid roofs; masts across the river hung with drooping half-furled sails; masts afar down thin and attenuated, mere dark straight lines in the distance. They await in stillness the rising of the tide." Richard Jefferies in "Nature near London."

UNDERGROUND

THE WAY OF BUSINESS

LONDON DOCKS AT WAPPING OR ROTHERHITHE STATIONS

THE WESTMINSTER PRESS

3 *The Way of Business* **Frank Brangwyn** 1913

4 *Winter's Discontent Made Glorious* **Artist unknown** 1909

The Trees

The trees are coming into leaf
Like something almost being said;
The recent buds relax and spread,
Their greenness is a kind of grief.

Is it that they are born again
And we grow old? No, they die too.
Their yearly trick of looking new
Is written down in rings of grain.

Yet still the unresting castles thresh
In fullgrown thickness every May.
Last year is dead, they seem to say,
Begin afresh, afresh, afresh.

PHILIP LARKIN (1922–85)

Benediction

Thanks to the ear
that someone may hear

Thanks to seeing
that someone may see

Thanks to feeling
that someone may feel

Thanks to touch
that one may be touched

Thanks to flowering of white moon
and spreading shawl of black night
holding villages and cities together

JAMES BERRY (b. 1924)

The Sick Rose

O Rose thou art sick.
The invisible worm
That flies in the night
In the howling storm,

Has found out thy bed
Of crimson joy:
And his dark secret love
Does thy life destroy.

WILLIAM BLAKE (1757–1827)

'Much Madness is divinest Sense'

Much Madness is divinest Sense –
To a discerning Eye –
Much Sense – the starkest Madness –
'Tis the Majority
In this, as All, prevail –
Assent – and you are sane –
Demur – you're straightway dangerous –
And handled with a Chain –

EMILY DICKINSON (1830–86)

At Lord's

It is little I repair to the matches of the Southron folk,
   Though my own red roses there may blow;
It is little I repair to the matches of the Southron folk,
   Though the red roses crest the caps, I know.
For the field is full of shades as I near the shadowy coast,
And a ghostly batsman plays to the bowling of a ghost,
And I look through my tears on a soundless-clapping host
   As the run-stealers flicker to and fro,
      To and fro: –
  O my Hornby and my Barlow long ago!

FRANCIS THOMPSON (1859–1907)

Rainforest

The forest drips and glows with green.
The tree-frog croaks his far-off song.
His voice is stillness, moss and rain
drunk from the forest ages long.

We cannot understand that call
unless we move into his dream,
where all is one and one is all
and frog and python are the same.

We with our quick dividing eyes
measure, distinguish and are gone.
The forest burns, the tree-frog dies,
yet one is all and all are one.

JUDITH WRIGHT (b. 1915)

Encounter at St. Martin's

I tell a wanderer's tale, the same
I began long ago, a boy in a barn,
I am always lost in it. The place
is always strange to me. In my pocket

the wrong money or none, the wrong paper,
maps of another town, the phrase book
for yesterday's language, just a ticket
to the next station, and my instructions.

In the lobby of the Banco Bilbao
a dark woman will slip me a key, a package,
the name of a hotel, a numbered account,
the first letters of an unknown alphabet.

KEN SMITH (b. 1938)

'Western wind when wilt thou blow'

Western wind when wilt thou blow
the small rain down can rain
Christ if my love were in my arms
and I in my bed again

ANON. (early 16th century)

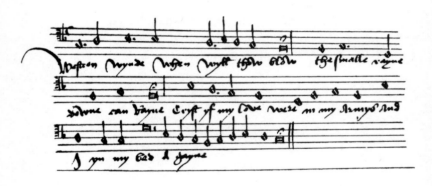

Westron wynde when wylt thou blow   Musical setting in a tenor part-book, dating from the early sixteenth century, which provides the only known source of this famous lyric. BL Royal MS, Appendix 58, f.5. By permission of The British Library Board.

Composed upon Westminster Bridge, September 3, 1802

Earth has not anything to show more fair:
Dull would he be of soul who could pass by
A sight so touching in its majesty:
This City now doth like a garment wear
The beauty of the morning; silent, bare,
Ships, towers, domes, theatres, and temples lie
Open unto the fields, and to the sky;
All bright and glittering in the smokeless air.
Never did sun more beautifully steep
In his first splendour valley, rock, or hill;
Ne'er saw I, never felt, a calm so deep!
The river glideth at his own sweet will:
Dear God! the very houses seem asleep;
And all that mighty heart is lying still!

WILLIAM WORDSWORTH (1770–1850)

Everyone Sang

Everyone suddenly burst out singing;
And I was filled with such delight
As prisoned birds must find in freedom,
Winging wildly across the white
Orchards and dark-green fields; on – on – and out of sigh

Everyone's voice was suddenly lifted;
And beauty came like the setting sun:
My heart was shaken with tears; and horror
Drifted away . . . O, but Everyone
Was a bird; and the song was wordless; the singing will
    be done.

April 1919

SIEGFRIED SASSOON (1886–1967)

The Loch Ness Monster's Song

Sssnnnwhuffffll?
Hnwhuffl hhnnwfl hnfl hfl?
Gdroblboblhobngbl gbl gl g g g g glbgl.
Drublhaflablhaflubhafgabhaflhafl fl fl –
gm grawwwww grf grawf awfgm graw gm.
Hovoplodok-doplodovok-plovodokot-doplodokosh?
Splgraw fok fok splgrafhatchgabrlgabrl fok splfok!
Zgra kra gka fok!
Grof grawff gahf?
Gombl mbl bl –
blm plm,
blm plm,
blm plm,
blp.

EDWIN MORGAN (b. 1920)

Living

The fire in leaf and grass
so green it seems
each summer the last summer.

The wind blowing, the leaves
shivering in the sun,
each day the last day.

A red salamander
so cold and so
easy to catch, dreamily

moves his delicate feet
and long tail. I hold
my hand open for him to go.

Each minute the last minute.

DENISE LEVERTOV (b. 1923)

Holy Sonnet

Death be not proud, though some have called thee
Mighty and dreadful, for thou art not so;
For those whom thou think'st thou dost overthrow
Die not, poor death, nor yet canst thou kill me.
From rest and sleep, which but thy pictures be,
Much pleasure, then from thee much more must flow;
And soonest our best men with thee do go,
Rest of their bones, and souls' delivery.
Thou art slave to Fate, chance, kings, and desperate men,
And dost with poison, war, and sickness dwell,
And poppy or charms can make us sleep as well,
And better than thy stroke; why swell'st thou then?
One short sleep past, we wake eternally,
And death shall be no more, Death thou shalt die.

JOHN DONNE (1572–1631)

'Trail all your pikes'

Trail all your pikes, dispirit every drum,
March in a slow procession from afar,
Ye silent, ye dejected men of war!
Be still the hautboys, and the flute be dumb!
Display no more, in vain, the lofty banner.
For see! where on the bier before ye lies
The pale, the fall'n, th'untimely sacrifice
To your mistaken shrine, to your false idol Honour!

from ALL IS VANITY

ANNE FINCH, Countess of Winchilsea (1661–1720)

Alas, Alack!

Ann, Ann!
   Come! quick as you can!
There's a fish that *talks*
   In the frying-pan.
Out of the fat,
   As clear as glass,
He put up his mouth
   And moaned 'Alas!'
Oh, most mournful,
   'Alas, alack!'
Then turned to his sizzling,
   And sank him back.

WALTER DE LA MARE (1873–1956)

Alas, Alack! Drawing by W. Heath Robinson, © The Estate of Mrs J. C. Robinson. By permission of Laurence Pollinger.

Immigrant

November '63: eight months in London.
I pause on the low bridge to watch the pelicans:
they float swanlike, arching their white necks
over only slightly ruffled bundles of wings,
burying awkward beaks in the lake's water.

I clench cold fists in my Marks and Spencer's jacket
and secretly test my accent once again:
St James's Park; St James's Park; St James's Park.

FLEUR ADCOCK (b. 1934)

I Am Becoming My Mother

Yellow/brown woman
fingers smelling always of onions

My mother raises rare blooms
and waters them with tea
her birth waters sang like rivers
my mother is now me

My mother had a linen dress
the colour of the sky
and stored lace and damask
tablecloths
to pull shame out of her eye.

I am becoming my mother
brown/yellow woman
fingers smelling always of onions.

LORNA GOODISON (b. 1947)

'Tagus farewell'

Tagus farewell, that westward with thy streams
Turns up the grains of gold already tried:
With spur and sail for I go seek the Thames
Gainward the sun that showeth her wealthy pride
And to the town which Brutus sought by dreams
Like bended moon doth lend her lusty side.
My king, my country, alone for whom I live,
Of mighty love the wings for this me give.

SIR THOMAS WYATT (1503–42)

'Tagus farewell'   A rare example of a poem in the author's hand, in a
handsome leatherbound notebook he kept from 1537 to 1542, which contains
over one hundred poems by Wyatt and several by the Earl of Surrey, most of
them in the hand of an amanuensis. The notebook was also used for drafts of
letters and mathematical computations over a period of one hundred years.
BL Egerton 2711, f.69. By permission of The British Library Board.

Snow

In the gloom of whiteness,
In the great silence of snow,
A child was sighing
And bitterly saying: 'Oh,
They have killed a white bird up there on her nest,
The down is fluttering from her breast!'
And still it fell through that dusky brightness
On the child crying for the bird of the snow.

EDWARD THOMAS (1878–1917)

Endymion Book 1st

A thing of beauty is a joy for ever:
Its loveliness increases; it will never
Pass into nothingness; but still will keep
A Bower quiet for us, and a sleep
Full of sweet dreams, and health, and quiet breathing.
Therefore, on every morrow, are we wreathing
A flowery band to bind us to the earth,
Spite of Despondence, of the inhuman dearth
Of noble natures, of the gloomy days,
Of all the unhealthy and oer-darkened ways
Made for our searching: yes, in spite of all
Some shape of beauty moves away the Pall
From our dark spirits. ~~and before us danceth~~
~~Lilies glitter on the point of Actaeon's Lances.~~

Endymion   The opening lines of the autograph fair copy, with Keats's corrections.
MA 208. By permission of The Pierpont Morgan Library, New York.

Lines *from* Endymion

A thing of beauty is a joy for ever:
Its loveliness increases; it will never
Pass into nothingness; but still will keep
A bower quiet for us, and a sleep
Full of sweet dreams, and health, and quiet breathing.
Therefore, on every morrow, are we wreathing
A flowery band to bind us to the earth,
Spite of despondence, of the inhuman dearth
Of noble natures, of the gloomy days,
Of all the unhealthy and o'er-darkened ways
Made for our searching: yes, in spite of all,
Some shape of beauty moves away the pall
From our dark spirits.

JOHN KEATS (1795–1821)

Celia Celia

When I am sad and weary
When I think all hope has gone
When I walk along High Holborn
I think of you with nothing on

ADRIAN MITCHELL (b. 1932)

Goodbye

He breathed in air, he breathed out light.
Charlie Parker was my delight.

ADRIAN MITCHELL

Ragwort

They won't let railways alone, those yellow flowers.
They're that remorseless joy of dereliction
darkest banks exhale like vivid breath
as bricks divide to let them root between.
How every falling place concocts their smile,
taking what's left and making a song of it.

ANNE STEVENSON (b. 1933)

'The silver swan'

The silver swan, who living had no note,
When death approached unlocked her silent throat,
Leaning her breast against the reedy shore,
Thus sung her first and last, and sung no more:
Farewell all joys, O death come close mine eyes,
More geese than swans now live, more fools than wise.

ANON. (*c.* 1600)

The silver Swanne   A setting by the court composer Orlando Gibbons of
this anonymous elegiac poem, in *The First Set of Madrigals and Mottets* (1612).
It has been suggested that the poem may refer to the death of Edmund
Spenser, in 1599. BL Royal Mus. 15.e.2 (10). By permission of The British
Library Board.

'So we'll go no more a-roving'

So we'll go no more a-roving
    So late into the night,
Though the heart be still as loving,
    And the moon be still as bright.

For the sword outwears its sheath,
    And the soul wears out the breast,
And the heart must pause to breathe,
    And Love itself have rest.

Though the night was made for loving,
    And the day returns too soon,
Yet we'll go no more a-roving
    By the light of the moon.

GEORGE GORDON, LORD BYRON (1788–1824)

Teeth

English Teeth, English Teeth!
Shining in the sun
A part of British heritage
Aye, each and every one.

English Teeth, Happy Teeth!
Always having fun
Clamping down on bits of fish
And sausages half done.

English Teeth! HEROES' Teeth!
Hear them click! and clack!
Let's sing a song of praise to them –
Three Cheers for the Brown Grey and Black.

SPIKE MILLIGAN (b. 1918)

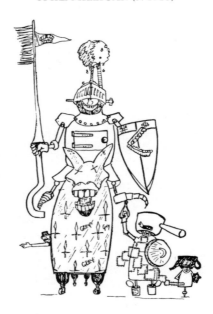

Teeth   Drawing by the author, in *Silly Verse for Kids* © Spike Milligan,
by permission of Spike Milligan Productions.

To My First White Hairs

Hirsute hell chimney-spouts, black thunderthroes
confluence of coarse cloudfleeces – my head sir! – scourbrush
in bitumen, past fossil beyond fingers of light – until . . .!

Sudden sprung as corn stalk after rain, watered milk weak;
as lightning shrunk to ant's antenna, shrivelled
off the febrile sight of crickets in the sun –

THREE WHITE HAIRS! frail invaders of the undergrowth
interpret time. I view them, wired wisps, vibrant coiled
beneath a magnifying glass, milk-thread presages

Of the hoary phase. Weave then, weave o quickly weave
your sham veneration. Knit me webs of winter sagehood,
nightcap, and the fungoid sequins of a crown.

WOLE SOYINKA (b. 1935)

Riddle-Me-Ree

My first is in life (not contained within heart)
My second's in whole but never in part.
My third's in forever, but also in vain.
My last's in ending, why not in pain?

is love the answer?

LIZ LOCHHEAD (b. 1947)

The Expulsion from Eden

In either hand the hast'ning angel caught
Our ling'ring parents, and to th' eastern gate
Led them direct, and down the cliff as fast
To the subjected plain; then disappeared.
They looking back, all th' eastern side beheld
Of Paradise, so late their happy seat,
Waved over by that flaming brand, the gate
With dreadful faces thronged and fiery arms:
Some natural tears they dropped, but wiped them soon;
The world was all before them, where to choose
Their place of rest, and Providence their guide:
They hand in hand with wand'ring steps and slow,
Through Eden took their solitary way.

from PARADISE LOST, BOOK XII

JOHN MILTON (1608–74)

'There was an Old Man with a beard'

There was an Old Man with a beard,
Who said, "It is just as I feared! –
  Two Owls and a Hen,
  Four Larks and a Wren,
Have all built their nests in my beard!"
from THE BOOK OF NONSENSE

EDWARD LEAR (1812–88)

There was an Old Man with a beard   Drawing by the author, from
The Book of Nonsense

Spring and Fall

to a young child

Margaret, are you grieving
Over Goldengrove unleaving?
Leaves, like the things of man, you
With your fresh thoughts care for, can you?
Ah! as the heart grows older
It will come to such sights colder
By and by, nor spare a sigh
Though worlds of wanwood leafmeal lie;
And yet you *will* weep and know why.
Now no matter, child, the name:
Sorrow's springs are the same.
Nor mouth had, no nor mind, expressed
What heart heard of, ghost guessed:
It is the blight man was born for,
It is Margaret you mourn for.

GERARD MANLEY HOPKINS (1844–89)

Dog Days

'When you stop to consider
The days spent dreaming of a future
And say then, that was my life.'

For the days are long –
From the first milk van
To the last shout in the night,
An eternity. But the weeks go by
Like birds; and the years, the years
Fly past anti-clockwise
Like clock hands in a bar mirror.

DEREK MAHON (b. 1941)

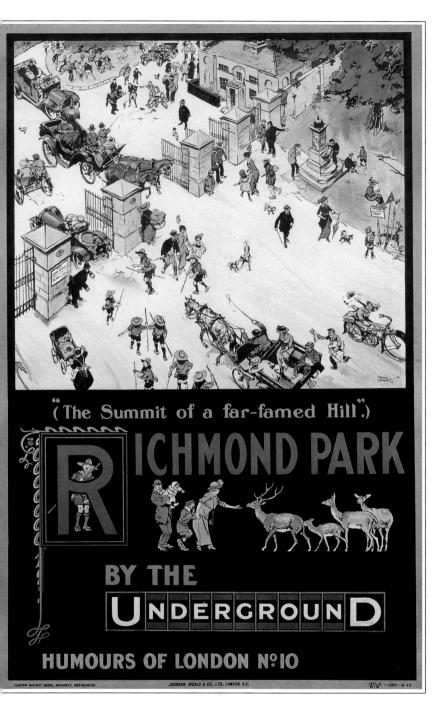

5 *Richmond Park* **Tony Sarg** 1913

6 *Fancy Dress* **Tony Sarg** 1913

7 *In Toyland* **Tony Sarg** 1913

8 *At Southend* **Tony Sarg** 1913

The Visitor

In Spanish he whispers there is no time left.
It is the sound of scythes arcing in wheat,
the ache of some field song in Salvador.
The wind along the prison, cautious
as Francisco's hands on the inside, touching
the walls as he walks, it is his wife's breath
slipping into his cell each night while he
imagines his hand to be hers. It is a small country.

There is nothing one man will not do to another.

CAROLYN FORCHÉ (b. 1950)

Ariel's Song

Full fathom five thy father lies,
   Of his bones are coral made:
Those are pearls that were his eyes,
   Nothing of him that doth fade,
But doth suffer a sea-change
Into something rich, and strange:
Sea-nymphs hourly ring his knell –
   Hark! now I hear them,
      Ding-dong bell.

from THE TEMPEST

WILLIAM SHAKESPEARE (1564–1616)

Ariel   Illustration by Arthur Rackham

Meeting at Night

The grey sea and the long black land;
And the yellow half-moon large and low;
And the startled little waves that leap
In fiery ringlets from their sleep,
As I gain the cove with pushing prow,
And quench its speed i' the slushy sand.

Then a mile of warm sea-scented beach;
Three fields to cross till a farm appears;
A tap at the pane, the quick sharp scratch
And blue spurt of a lighted match,
And a voice less loud, thro' its joys and fears,
Than the two hearts beating each to each!

ROBERT BROWNING (1812–89)

Prelude I

The winter evening settles down
With smell of steaks in passageways.
Six o'clock.
The burnt-out ends of smoky days.
And now a gusty shower wraps
The grimy scraps
Of withered leaves about your feet
And newspapers from vacant lots;
The showers beat
On broken blinds and chimney-pots,
And at the corner of the street
A lonely cab-horse steams and stamps.

And then the lighting of the lamps.

T. S. ELIOT (1888–1965)

London Airport

Last night in London Airport
I saw a wooden bin
labelled UNWANTED LITERATURE
IS TO BE PLACED HEREIN.
So I wrote a poem
and popped it in.

CHRISTOPHER LOGUE (b. 1926)

Taid's Grave

Rain on lilac leaves. In the dusk
they show me the grave,
a casket of stars underfoot,
his name there, and his language.

Voice of thrushes in rain.
My cousin Gwynfor eases me
into the green cave.
Wet hands of lilac

touch my wrist and the secret
unfreckled underside of my arm
daring fingers to count
five warm blue eggs.

GILLIAN CLARKE (b. 1937)

Taid: Welsh for grandfather.

The Coming of Grendel

Now from the marshlands under the mist-mountains
Came Grendel prowling; branded with God's ire.
This murderous monster was minded to entrap
Some hapless human in that high hall.
On he came under the clouds, until clearly
He could see the great golden feasting place,
Glimmering wine-hall of men. Not his first
Raid was this on the homeplace of Hrothgar.
Never before though and never afterward
Did he encounter hardier defenders of a hall.

from BEOWULF (10th century or earlier)

translated by GERARD BENSON

In my Craft or Sullen Art

In my craft or sullen art
Exercised in the still night
When only the moon rages
And the lovers lie abed
With all their griefs in their arms,
I labour by singing light
Not for ambition or bread
Or the strut and trade of charms
On the ivory stages
But for the common wages
Of their most secret heart.

Not for the proud man apart
From the raging moon I write
On these spindrift pages
Nor for the towering dead
With their nightingales and psalms
But for the lovers, their arms
Round the griefs of the ages,
Who pay no praise or wages
Nor heed my craft or art.

DYLAN THOMAS (1914–53)

Midsummer, Tobago

Broad sun-stoned beaches.

White heat.
A green river.

A bridge,
scorched yellow palms

from the summer-sleeping house
drowsing through August.

Days I have held,
days I have lost,

days that outgrow, like daughters,
my harbouring arms.

DEREK WALCOTT (b. 1930)

How do I love thee? Autograph manuscript, with corrections, of one of the most popular 'Sonnets from the Portuguese'. BL Add. MS 43487, f.49. By permission of The British Library Board.

Sonnet from the Portuguese

How do I love thee? Let me count the ways.
I love thee to the depth and breadth and height
My soul can reach, when feeling out of sight
For the ends of Being and ideal Grace.
I love thee to the level of everyday's
Most quiet need, by sun and candlelight.
I love thee freely, as men strive for Right;
I love thee purely, as they turn from Praise.
I love thee with the passion put to use
In my old griefs, and with my childhood's faith.
I love thee with a love I seemed to lose
With my lost saints, – I love thee with the breath,
Smiles, tears, of all my life! – and, if God choose,
I shall but love thee better after death.

ELIZABETH BARRETT BROWNING (1806–61)

Handbag

My mother's old leather handbag,
crowded with letters she carried
all through the war. The smell
of my mother's handbag: mints
and lipstick and Coty powder.
The look of those letters, softened
and worn at the edges, opened,
read, and refolded so often.
Letters from my father. Odour
of leather and powder, which ever
since then has meant womanliness,
and love, and anguish, and war.

RUTH FAINLIGHT (b. 1931)

Symphony in Yellow

An omnibus across the bridge
   Crawls like a yellow butterfly,
   And, here and there, a passer-by
Shows like a little restless midge.

Big barges full of yellow hay
   Are moored against the shadowy wharf,
   And, like a yellow silken scarf,
The thick fog hangs along the quay.

The yellow leaves begin to fade
   And flutter from the Temple elms,
   And at my feet the pale green Thames
Lies like a rod of rippled jade.

OSCAR WILDE (1854–1900)

Caricature of Oscar Wilde
in a Top Hat. Black and white
drawing by Beatrice Whistler.
Birnie Philip Bequest. By
permission of The Hunterian
Art Gallery, University of
Glasgow.

77

'Sumer is icumen in' English and Latin texts, with music, of the earliest known English round. The Latin text is completely unrelated to the English original. From a manuscript transcribed at Reading Abbey in the early thirteenth century. BL Harley 978. f.11v. By permission of The British Library Board.

'Sumer is icumen in'

Sumer is icumen in,
Loud sing cuckoo!
Groweth seed and bloweth mead
And springeth the wood now.
Sing cuckoo!

Ewe bleateth after lamb,
Cow loweth after calf,
Bullock starteth, buck farteth,
Merry sing cuckoo!

Cuckoo, cuckoo!
Well singest thou cuckoo,
Nor cease thou never now!

Sing cuckoo now, sing cuckoo!
Sing cuckoo, sing cuckoo now!

ANON. (13th century)

Song

Stop all the clocks, cut off the telephone,
Prevent the dog from barking with a juicy bone,
Silence the pianos and with muffled drum
Bring out the coffin, let the mourners come.

Let aeroplanes circle moaning overhead
Scribbling on the sky the message He Is Dead,
Put crêpe bows round the white necks of the public doves,
Let the traffic policemen wear black cotton gloves.

He was my North, my South, my East and West,
My working week and my Sunday rest,
My noon, my midnight, my talk, my song;
I thought that love would last for ever: I was wrong.

The stars are not wanted now; put out every one,
Pack up the moon and dismantle the sun,
Pour away the ocean and sweep up the wood;
For nothing now can ever come to any good.

W. H. AUDEN (1907–73)

The Ancients of the World

The salmon lying in the depths of Llyn Llifon,
   Secretly as a thought in a dark mind,
Is not so old as the owl of Cwm Cowlyd
   Who tells her sorrow nightly on the wind.

The ousel singing in the woods of Cilgwri,
   Tirelessly as a stream over the mossed stones,
Is not so old as the toad of Cors Fochno
   Who feels the cold skin sagging round his bones.

The toad and the ousel and the stag of Rhedynfre,
   That has cropped each leaf from the tree of life,
Are not so old as the owl of Cwm Cowlyd,
   That the proud eagle would have to wife.

R. S. THOMAS (b. 1913)

Day Trip

Two women, seventies, hold hands
on the edge of Essex,
hair in strong nets,
shrieked laughter echoing gulls
as shingle sucks from under feet
easing in brine.

There must be an unspoken point
when the sea feels like
their future. No longer paddling,
ankles submerge in lace,
in satin ripple.
Dress hems darken.

They do not risk their balance
for the shimmering of ships
at the horizon's sweep
as, thigh deep, they inch on
fingers splayed, wrists bent,
learning to walk again.

CAROLE SATYAMURTI (b. 1939)

In Time of 'The Breaking of Nations'

I

Only a man harrowing clods
   In a slow silent walk
With an old horse that stumbles and nods
   Half asleep as they stalk.

II

Only thin smoke without flame
   From the heaps of couch-grass;
Yet this will go onward the same
   Though Dynasties pass.

III

Yonder a maid and her wight
   Come whispering by:
War's annals will cloud into night
   Ere their story die.

THOMAS HARDY (1840–1928)

'Thou art my battle axe and weapons of war: for with thee will I break in pieces the nations, and with thee will I destroy kingdoms' (Jeremiah: 51.20).

London Bells

Two sticks and an apple,
Ring the bells at Whitechapel.

Old Father Bald Pate,
Ring the bells Aldgate.

Maids in white aprons,
Ring the bells at St. Catherine's.

Oranges and lemons,
Ring the bells at St. Clement's.

When will you pay me?
Ring the bells at the Old Bailey.

When I am rich,
Ring the bells at Fleetditch.

When will that be?
Ring the bells at Stepney.

When I am old,
Ring the great bell at Paul's.

ANON. (early 18th century)

London Bells.

Two Sticks & an Apple,
Ring ẙ Bells at Whitechapple
Old Father Bald Pate,
Ring ẙ Bells Aldgate ,
Maids in white Aprons,
Ring ẙ Bells a S.ᵗCathrines,
          Oranges

Oranges and Lemmons,
Ring ẙ Bells at S.ᵗClemens,
When will you pay me,
Ring ẙ Bells at ẙ Old Bailey,
When I am Rich,
Ring ẙ Bells at Fleetditch,
When will that be,
Ring ẙ Bells at Stepney,
When I am Old,
Ring ẙ great Bell at Pauls .

London Bells   The traditional London rhyme as it appears in an early hand-set printed children's book, *Tommy Thumb's Pretty Song Book* (1744), Vol. II. By permission of The British Library Board.

The Tyger   A much-corrected autograph draft of the poem, in Blake's notebook, the 'Rossetti Manuscript'. BL Add. MS 49460, f.56. By permission of The British Library Board .

The Tyger

Tyger Tyger, burning bright,
In the forests of the night;
What immortal hand or eye,
Could frame thy fearful symmetry?

In what distant deeps or skies
Burnt the fire of thine eyes!
On what wings dare he aspire?
What the hand, dare sieze the fire?

And what shoulder, & what art,
Could twist the sinews of thy heart?
And when thy heart began to beat,
What dread hand? & what dread feet?

What the hammer? what the chain?
In what furnace was thy brain?
What the anvil? what dread grasp,
Dare its deadly terrors clasp?

When the stars threw down their spears
And water'd heaven with their tears:
Did he smile his work to see?
Did he who made the Lamb make thee?

Tyger Tyger, burning bright,
In the forests of the night:
What immortal hand or eye,
Dare frame thy fearful symmetry?

WILLIAM BLAKE (1757–1827)

Delay

The radiance of that star that leans on me
Was shining years ago. The light that now
Glitters up there my eye may never see,
And so the time lag teases me with how

Love that loves now may not reach me until
Its first desire is spent. The star's impulse
Must wait for eyes to claim it beautiful
And love arrived may find us somewhere else.

ELIZABETH JENNINGS (b. 1926)

Everything Changes

after Brecht, *'Alles wandelt sich'*

Everything changes. We plant
trees for those born later
but what's happened has happened,
and poisons poured into the seas
cannot be drained out again.

What's happened has happened.
Poisons poured into the seas
cannot be drained out again, but
everything changes. We plant
trees for those born later.

CICELY HERBERT (b. 1937)

Roundel

Now welcome Summer with thy sunnė soft,
That hast this winter's weathers overshake,
And driven away the longė nightės black.

Saint Valentine, that art full high aloft,
Thus singen smallė fowlės for thy sake:
Now welcome Summer with thy sunnė soft,
That hast this winter's weathers overshake.

Well have they cause for to gladden oft,
Since each of them recovered hath his make.
Full blissful may they singė when they wake:
Now welcome Summer with thy sunnė soft,
That hast this winter's weathers overshake,
And driven away the longė nightės black!

from THE PARLIAMENT OF FOWLS

GEOFFREY CHAUCER (1340?–1400)

Introduction to *The Parliament of Fowls* from a fifteenth-century copy of
Chaucer's Works in the Cambridge University Library. GG.4.27, f.480b. By
permission of the Syndics of Cambridge University Library.

Dreams

Here we are all, by day; by night we're hurled
By dreams, each one, into a several world.

ROBERT HERRICK (1591–1674)

Sonnet

What lips my lips have kissed, and where, and why,
I have forgotten, and what arms have lain
Under my head till morning; but the rain
Is full of ghosts tonight, that tap and sigh
Upon the glass and listen for reply,
And in my heart there stirs a quiet pain
For unremembered lads that not again
Will turn to me at midnight with a cry.
Thus in the winter stands the lonely tree,
Nor knows what birds have vanished one by one,
Yet knows its boughs more silent than before:
I cannot say what loves have come and gone,
I only know that summer sang in me
A little while, that in me sings no more.

EDNA ST. VINCENT MILLAY (1892–1950)

And Yet the Books

And yet the books will be there on the shelves, separate beings,
That appeared once, still wet
As shining chestnuts under a tree in autumn,
And, touched, coddled, began to live
In spite of fires on the horizon, castles blown up,
Tribes on the march, planets in motion.
"We are," they said, even as their pages
Were being torn out, or a buzzing flame
Licked away their letters. So much more durable
Than we are, whose frail warmth
Cools down with memory, disperses, perishes.
I imagine the earth when I am no more:
Nothing happens, no loss, it's still a strange pageant,
Women's dresses, dewy lilacs, a song in the valley.
Yet the books will be there on the shelves, well born,
Derived from people, but also from radiance, heights.

CZESLAW MILOSZ (b. 1911)
translated by CZESLAW MILOSZ *and* ROBERT HASS

The Leader

I wanna be the leader
I wanna be the leader
Can I be the leader?
Can I? I can?
Promise? Promise?
Yippee, I'm the leader
I'm the leader

OK what shall we do?

ROGER McGOUGH (b. 1937)

from To the City of London

Above all rivers thy river hath renown,
Whose beryl streamės, pleasant and preclare,
Under thy lusty wallės runneth down;
Where many a swan doth swim with wingės fair,
Where many a barge doth sail, and row with oar,
Where many a ship doth rest with top-royal.
O town of townės, patron and not compare,
London, thou art the flower of Cities all.

WILLIAM DUNBAR (1465?–1530?)

To the City of London   The 'river' stanza. The full text of the poem is
copied into *The Chronicle of London 1215–1509*, where the poem is said to have
been 'made' while the company was sitting at dinner. BL Cotton MS Vitell.
A.XVI, f.200v. By permission of The British Library Board.

On First Looking into Chapman's Homer

Much have I travell'd in the realms of gold,
   And many goodly states and kingdoms seen;
   Round many western islands have I been
Which bards in fealty to Apollo hold.
Oft of one wide expanse had I been told
   That deep-brow'd Homer ruled as his demesne;
   Yet did I never breathe its pure serene
Till I heard Chapman speak out loud and bold:
Then felt I like some watcher of the skies
   When a new planet swims into his ken;
Or like stout Cortez when with eagle eyes
   He star'd at the Pacific – and all his men
Look'd at each other with a wild surmise –
   Silent, upon a peak in Darien.

JOHN KEATS (1795–1821)

DORKING
BY MOTOR-BUS

"I know these slopes: who knows them if not I?
  Many a dingle on the loved hill-side.
With thorns once studded, old, white blossom'd trees
  Where thick the cowslips grew, and far descried
High tower'd the spikes of purple orchises."

Matthew Arnold.

DANGERFIELD PRINTING CO LTD LONDON. 65. LOGO. 5/2/20.　　　　　　ELECTRIC RAILWAY HOUSE, BROADWAY, WESTMINSTER. S.W.

9 *Dorking by Motor-Bus* **F. Gregory Brown** 1920

WOTTON CHURCH, NEAR DORKING

O sweeter than the marriage-feast,
'Tis sweeter far to me,
To walk together to the kirk
With a goodly company! —

To walk together to the kirk,
And all together pray,
While each to his great Father bends,
Old men, and babes, and loving friends,
And youths and maidens gay!

SAMUEL TAYLOR COLERIDGE

10 *Wotton Church ('O sweeter than the marriage-feast')* **Adrian Allinson** 1940

11 *Rambling Parties ('Away to the green, green country')* **A.E.Marty** 1931

All things above were bright and fair,
All things were glad and free;
The squirrels darted here and there,
And wild birds filled the echoing air
With songs of liberty!   LONGFELLOW.

12 *'All things above were bright and fair'* **Ethelbert White** 1927

A Dead Statesman

I could not dig: I dared not rob:
Therefore I lied to please the mob.
Now all my lies are proved untrue
And I must face the men I slew.
What tale shall serve me here among
Mine angry and defrauded young?

from EPITAPHS OF THE WAR 1914–18

RUDYARD KIPLING (1865–1936)

Modern Secrets

Last night I dreamt in Chinese.
Eating Yankee shredded wheat
I said it in English
To a friend who answered
In monosyllables:
All of which I understood.

The dream shrank to its fiction.
I had understood its end
Many years ago. The sallow child
Ate rice from its ricebowl
And hides still in the cupboard
With the china and tea-leaves.

SHIRLEY GEOK-LIN LIM (b. 1944)

Sergeant Brown's Parrot

Many policemen wear upon their shoulders
Cunning little radios. To pass away the time
They talk about the traffic to them, listen to the news,
And it helps them to Keep Down Crime.

But Sergeant Brown, he wears upon his shoulder
A tall green parrot as he's walking up and down
And all the parrot says is "Who's-a-pretty-boy-then?"
"I am," says Sergeant Brown.

KIT WRIGHT (b. 1944)

Sergeant Brown's Parrot   Drawing by Posy Simmonds, © Posy
Simmonds. By permission of Collins Publishers.

'I have a gentil cock'

I have a gentil cock, croweth me day
he doth me risen early, my matins for to say

I have a gentil cock, comen he is of great
his comb is of red coral, his tail is of jet

I have a gentil cock, comen he is of kind
his comb is of red sorrel, his tail is of inde

his legs be of azure, so gentil and so small
his spurs are of silver white, into the wortewale

his eyes are of crystal, locked all in amber
and every night he percheth him in my lady's chamber

ANON. (early 15th century)

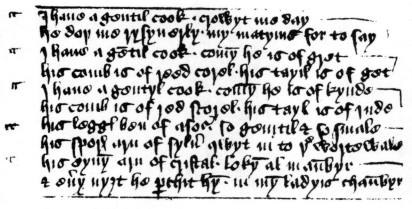

'I have a gentil cook [cock]'   From a collection dating from the early
15th century, and attributed to the monastery of Bury St Edmunds, containing
the only surviving copies of over 70 early English carols and other lyrics.
BL MS Sloane 2593, f.10b. By permission of The British Library Board.

What Am I After All

What am I after all but a child, pleas'd with the sound of
    my own name? repeating it over and over;
I stand apart to hear – it never tires me.

To you your name also;
Did you think there was nothing but two or three
    pronunciations in the sound of your name?

WALT WHITMAN (1819–92)

Piano

Softly, in the dusk, a woman is singing to me;
Taking me back down the vista of years, till I see
A child sitting under the piano, in the boom of the tingling
    strings
And pressing the small, poised feet of a mother who smiles as
    she sings.

In spite of myself, the insidious mastery of song
Betrays me back, till the heart of me weeps to belong
To the old Sunday evenings at home, with winter outside
And hymns in the cosy parlour, the tinkling piano our guide.

So now it is vain for the singer to burst into clamour
With the great black piano appassionato. The glamour
Of childish days is upon me, my manhood is cast
Down in the flood of remembrance, I weep like a child for the
    past.

D. H. LAWRENCE (1885–1930)

Mmenson

Summon now the kings of the forest,
horn of the elephant,
mournful call of the elephant;

summon the emirs, kings of the desert,
horses caparisoned, beaten gold bent,
archers and criers, porcupine arrows, bows bent;

recount now the gains and the losses:
Agades, Sokoto, El Hassan dead in his tent,
the silks and the brasses, the slow weary tent

of our journeys down slopes, dry river courses;
land of the lion, land of the leopard, elephant
country; tall grasses, thick prickly herbs. Blow elephant

trumpet; summon the horses,
dead horses, our losses: the bent
slow bow of the Congo, the watering Niger . . .

EDWARD KAMAU BRATHWAITE (b. 1930)

Light

I live for books
and light to read them in.
                          Waterlilies
reaching up
from the depths of the pond
algae dark,
the frog loves a jell of
blue-green water,
                    the bud
scales
a rope of stem,
then floats in sunshine. Like soap
in the morning bath.
This book I read
floats in my hand like a waterlily
coming out of the nutrient waters
of thought
and light shines on us both,
the morning's breviary.

DIANE WAKOSKI (b. 1937)

from The Song of Solomon

My beloved spake, and said unto me, Rise up, my love, my fair
    one, and come away.
For lo, the winter is past, the rain is over, and gone.
The flowers appear on the earth, the time of the singing of
    birds is come, and the voice of the turtle is heard in our
    land.
The fig tree putteth forth her green figs, and the vines with
    the tender grape give a good smell.
Arise, my love, my fair one, and come away.

THE KING JAMES BIBLE (1611)

'You took away all the oceans and all the room'

You took away all the oceans and all the room.
You gave me my shoe-size in earth with bars around it.
Where did it get you? Nowhere.
You left me my lips, and they shape words, even in silence.

OSIP MANDELSTAM (1891–1938)
translated by CLARENCE BROWN *and* W. S. MERWIN

Wet Evening in April

The birds sang in the wet trees
And as I listened to them it was a hundred years from now
And I was dead and someone else was listening to them.
But I was glad I had recorded for him
   The melancholy.

PATRICK KAVANAGH (1906–67)

I Saw a Jolly Hunter

I saw a jolly hunter
  With a jolly gun
Walking in the country
  In the jolly sun.

In the jolly meadow
  Sat a jolly hare.
Saw the jolly hunter.
  Took jolly care.

Hunter jolly eager –
  Sight of jolly prey.
Forgot gun pointing
  Wrong jolly way.

Jolly hunter jolly head
  Over heels gone.
Jolly old safety catch
  Not jolly on.

Bang went the jolly gun.
  Hunter jolly dead.
Jolly hare got clean away.
  Jolly good, I said.

CHARLES CAUSLEY (b. 1917)

I Saw a Jolly Hunter   Drawing by
Pat Marriott, from *Figgie Hobbin*.
By permission of Macmillan London.

Aunt Jennifer's Tigers

Aunt Jennifer's tigers prance across a screen,
Bright topaz denizens of a world of green.
They do not fear the men beneath the tree;
They pace in sleek chivalric certainty.

Aunt Jennifer's fingers fluttering through her wool
Find even the ivory needle hard to pull.
The massive weight of Uncle's wedding band
Sits heavily upon Aunt Jennifer's hand.

When Aunt is dead, her terrified hands will lie
Still ringed with ordeals she was mastered by.
The tigers in the panel that she made
Will go on prancing, proud and unafraid.

ADRIENNE RICH (b. 1929)

Old English Riddle

A moth, I thought, munching a word.
How marvellously weird! a worm
Digesting a man's sayings –
A sneakthief nibbling in the shadows
At the shape of a poet's thunderous phrases –
How unutterably strange!
And the pilfering parasite none the wiser
For the words he has swallowed.

from THE EXETER BOOK
translated by GERARD BENSON

Answer: Bookworm

Old English Riddle from *The Exeter Book*, a manuscript of about the year 1000,
containing over ninety riddles and several other Old English poems. Reprinted
with the permission of the Dean and Chapter of Exeter Cathedral.

Virtue

Sweet day, so cool, so calm, so bright,
The bridal of the earth and sky:
The dew shall weep thy fall tonight;
                For thou must die.

Sweet rose, whose hue angry and brave
Bids the rash gazer wipe his eye:
Thy root is ever in its grave,
                And thou must die.

Sweet spring, full of sweet days and roses,
A box where sweets compacted lie;
My music shows ye have your closes,
                And all must die.

Only a sweet and virtuous soul,
Like seasoned timber, never gives;
But though the whole world turn to coal,
                Then chiefly lives.

GEORGE HERBERT (1593–1633)

'I know the truth – give up all other truths!'

I know the truth – give up all other truths!
No need for people anywhere on earth to struggle.
Look – it is evening, look, it is nearly night:
what do you speak of, poets, lovers, generals?

The wind is level now, the earth is wet with dew,
the storm of stars in the sky will turn to quiet.
And soon all of us will sleep under the earth, we
who never let each other sleep above it.

1915

MARINA TSVETAYEVA (1892–1941)
translated by ELAINE FEINSTEIN

Love Without Hope

Love without hope, as when the young bird-catcher
Swept off his tall hat to the Squire's own daughter,
So let the imprisoned larks escape and fly
Singing about her head, as she rode by.

ROBERT GRAVES (1895–1985)

Full Moon and Little Frieda

A cool small evening shrunk to a dog bark and the clank
                                   of a bucket –

And you listening.
A spider's web, tense for the dew's touch.
A pail lifted, still and brimming – mirror
To tempt a first star to a tremor.

Cows are going home in the lane there, looping the hedges
                    with their warm wreaths of breath –
A dark river of blood, many boulders,
Balancing unspilled milk.

'Moon!' you cry suddenly, 'Moon! Moon!'

The moon has stepped back like an artist gazing amazed
                                   at a work
That points at him amazed.

TED HUGHES (b. 1930)

'Since there's no help, come let us kiss and part'

Since there's no help, come let us kiss and part,
Nay, I have done: you get no more of me,
And I am glad, yea glad with all my heart
That thus so cleanly I myself can free,
Shake hands forever, cancel all our vows,
And when we meet at any time again,
Be it not seen in either of our brows
That we one jot of former love retain.
Now at the last gasp of love's latest breath,
When his pulse failing, passion speechless lies,
When faith is kneeling by his bed of death,
And innocence is closing up his eyes,
   Now if thou wouldst, when all have given him over,
   From death to life thou mightst him yet recover.

MICHAEL DRAYTON (1563–1631)

'Into my heart an air that kills'

Into my heart an air that kills
   From yon far country blows:
What are those blue remembered hills,
   What spires, what farms are those?

That is the land of lost content,
   I see it shining plain,
The happy highways where I went
   And cannot come again.

from A SHROPSHIRE LAD

A. E. HOUSMAN (1859–1936)

Dolor

I have known the inexorable sadness of pencils,
Neat in their boxes, dolor of pad and paper-weight,
All the misery of manilla folders and mucilage,
Desolation in immaculate public places,
Lonely reception room, lavatory, switchboard,
The unalterable pathos of basin and pitcher,
Ritual of multigraph, paper-clip, comma,
Endless duplication of lives and objects.
And I have seen dust from the walls of institutions,
Finer than flour, alive, more dangerous than silica,
Sift, almost invisible, through long afternoons of tedium,
Dropping a fine film on nails and delicate eyebrows,
Glazing the pale hair, the duplicate grey standard faces.

THEODORE ROETHKE (1908–63)

The Cries of London

Here's fine rosemary, sage, and thyme.
Come buy my ground ivy.
Here's fetherfew, gilliflowers and rue.
Come buy my knotted marjorum, ho!
Come buy my mint, my fine green mint.
Here's fine lavender for your cloaths.
Here's parsley and winter-savory,
And hearts-ease, which all do choose.
Here's balm and hissop, and cinquefoil,
All fine herbs, it is well known.
    Let none despise the merry, merry cries
    Of famous London-town!

Here's fine herrings, eight a groat.
Hot codlins, pies and tarts.
New mackerel! have to sell.
Come buy my Wellfleet oysters, ho!
Come buy my whitings fine and new.
Wives, shall I mend your husbands horns?
I'll grind your knives to please your wives,
And very nicely cut your corns.
Maids, have you any hair to sell,
Either flaxen, black, or brown?
    Let none despise the merry, merry cries
    Of famous London-town!

ANON. (17th century)

The Cries of London   A setting by Orlando Gibbons of several London 'Cries' for five singers and five viol players. BL. Add.MS 29373, f.33v. By permission of The British Library Board.

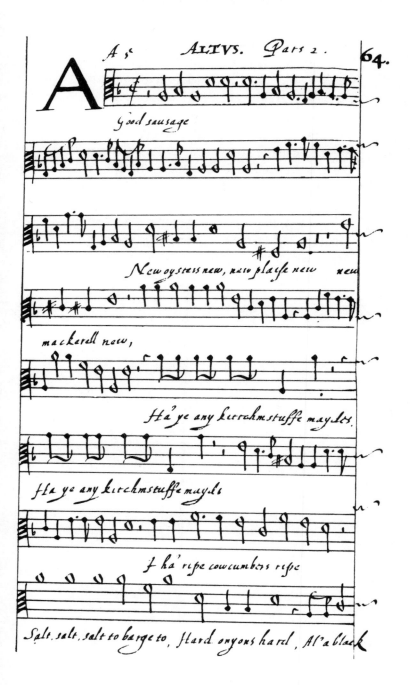

A 14-Year-Old Convalescent Cat in the Winter

I want him to have another living summer,
to lie in the sun and enjoy the *douceur de vivre* –
because the sun, like golden rum in a rummer,
is what makes an idle cat *un tout petit peu ivre* –

I want him to lie stretched out, contented,
revelling in the heat, his fur all dry and warm,
an Old Age Pensioner, retired, resented
by no one, and happinesses in a beelike swarm

to settle on him – postponed for another season
that last fated hateful journey to the vet
from which there is no return (and age the reason),
which must soon come – as I cannot forget.

GAVIN EWART (1916–95)

Come. And Be My Baby

The highway is full of big cars
going nowhere fast
And folks is smoking anything that'll burn
Some people wrap their lives around a cocktail glass
And you sit wondering
where you're going to turn.
I got it.
Come. And be my baby.

Some prophets say the world is gonna end tomorrow
But others say we've got a week or two
The paper is full of every kind of blooming horror
And you sit wondering
what you're gonna do.
I got it.
Come. And be my baby.

MAYA ANGELOU (b. 1928)

'Ich am of Irlonde'

I am of Ireland,
And of the holy land
Of Ireland.

Good sir, pray I thee,
For of saint charity,
Come and dance with me
In Ireland.

ANON. (14th century)

Song

Now sleeps the crimson petal, now the white;
Nor waves the cypress in the palace walk;
Nor winks the gold fin in the porphyry font:
The fire-fly wakens: waken thou with me.

Now droops the milkwhite peacock like a ghost,
And like a ghost she glimmers on to me.

Now lies the Earth all Danaë to the stars,
And all thy heart lies open unto me.

Now slides the silent meteor on, and leaves
A shining furrow, as thy thoughts in me.

Now folds the lily all her sweetness up,
And slips into the bosom of the lake:
So fold thyself, my dearest, thou, and slip
Into my bosom and be lost in me.

from THE PRINCESS

ALFRED, LORD TENNYSON (1809–92)

The Embankment

(The Fantasia of a Fallen Gentleman on a Cold, Bitter Night)

Once, in finesse of fiddles found I ecstasy,
In a flash of gold heels on the hard pavement.
Now see I
That warmth's the very stuff of poesy.
Oh, God, make small
The old star-eaten blanket of the sky,
That I may fold it round me and in comfort lie.

T. E. HULME (1883–1917)

Stars and planets

Trees are cages for them: water holds its breath
To balance them without smudging on its delicate meniscus.
Children watch them playing in their heavenly playground;
Men use them to lug ships across oceans, through firths.

They seem so twinkle-still, but they never cease
Inventing new spaces and huge explosions
And migrating in mathematical tribes over
The steppes of space at their outrageous ease.

It's hard to think that the earth is one –
This poor sad bearer of wars and disasters
Rolls-Roycing round the sun with its load of gangsters,
Attended only by the loveless moon.

NORMAN MacCAIG (1910–96)

The Uncertainty of the Poet

I am a poet.
I am very fond of bananas.

I am bananas.
I am very fond of a poet.

I am a poet of bananas.
I am very fond.

A fond poet of 'I am, I am' –
Very bananas.

Fond of 'Am I bananas?
Am I?' – a very poet.

Bananas of a poet!
Am I fond? Am I very?

Poet bananas! I am.
I am fond of a 'very'.

I am of very fond bananas.
Am I a poet?

WENDY COPE (b. 1945)

'I saw a Peacock with a fiery tail'

I saw a Peacock with a fiery tail
I saw a blazing Comet drop down hail
I saw a Cloud with Ivy circled round
I saw a sturdy Oak creep on the ground
I saw a Pismire swallow up a Whale
I saw a raging Sea brim full of Ale
I saw a Venice Glass sixteen foot deep
I saw a Well full of men's tears that weep
I saw their Eyes all in a flame of fire
I saw a House as big as the Moon and higher
I saw the Sun even in the midst of night
I saw the Man that saw this wondrous sight.

ANON. (17th century)

from **Frost at Midnight**

The Frost performs its secret ministry,
Unhelped by any wind. The owlet's cry
Came loud – and hark, again! loud as before.
The inmates of my cottage, all at rest,
Have left me to that solitude, which suits
Abstruser musings: save that at my side
My cradled infant slumbers peacefully.
'Tis calm indeed! so calm, that it disturbs
And vexes meditation with its strange
And extreme silentness. Sea, hill, and wood,
This populous village! Sea, and hill, and wood,
With all the numberless goings-on of life,
Inaudible as dreams!

SAMUEL TAYLOR COLERIDGE (1772–1834)

"...Search down the marge to find some shady pool
Where we may rest awhile and moor our boat,
And bathe our tired limbs in the waters cool...."

13 *River* **Clifford and Rosemary Ellis** 1933

14 *Wood* **Clifford and Rosemary Ellis** 1933

"I climb your crown, and lo! a sight surprising....."

GREEN·LINE

15 *Down* **Clifford and Rosemary Ellis** 1933

"Then the lone owl awoke from rest,
Stretch'd his keen talons, plum'd his crest,
And from his high embattl'd station,
Hooted a trembling salutation."

UNDERGROUND

16 *Heath* **Clifford and Rosemary Ellis** 1933

Snow

The room was suddenly rich and the great bay-window was
Spawning snow and pink roses against it
Soundlessly collateral and incompatible:
World is suddener than we fancy it.

World is crazier and more of it than we think,
Incorrigibly plural. I peel and portion
A tangerine and spit the pips and feel
The drunkenness of things being various.

And the fire flames with a bubbling sound for world
Is more spiteful and gay than one supposes –
On the tongue on the eyes on the ears in the palms of one's
    hands –
There is more than glass between the snow and the huge
    roses.

LOUIS MacNEICE (1907–63)

On Himself

Abstracted by silence from the age of seven,
Deafened and penned by as black calamity
As twice to be born, I cannot without pity
Contemplate myself as an infant;

Or fail to speak of silence as a priestess
Calling to serve in the temple of a skull
Her innocent choice. It is barely possible
Not to be affected by such a distress.

DAVID WRIGHT (1920–94)

Sometimes

Sometimes things don't go, after all,
from bad to worse. Some years, muscadel
faces down frost; green thrives; the crops don't fail,
sometimes a man aims high, and all goes well.

A people sometimes will step back from war;
elect an honest man; decide they care
enough, that they can't leave some stranger poor.
Some men become what they were born for.

Sometimes our best efforts do not go
amiss; sometimes we do as we meant to.
The sun will sometimes melt a field of sorrow
that seemed hard frozen: may it happen for you.

SHEENAGH PUGH (b. 1950)

The Passionate Shepherd to his Love

Come live with me, and be my love,
And we will all the pleasures prove
That valleys, groves, hills and fields,
Woods, or steepy mountain yields.

And we will sit upon the rocks,
Seeing the shepherds feed their flocks
By shallow rivers, to whose falls
Melodious birds sing madrigals.

And I will make thee beds of roses,
And a thousand fragrant posies,
A cap of flowers, and a kirtle,
Embroidered all with leaves of myrtle.

A gown made of the finest wool
Which from our pretty lambs we pull,
Fair lined slippers for the cold,
With buckles of the purest gold.

A belt of straw and ivy buds,
With coral clasps and amber studs,
And if these pleasures may thee move,
Come live with me, and be my love.

The shepherds' swains shall dance and sing
For thy delight each May-morning;
If these delights thy mind may move,
Then live with me, and be my love.

CHRISTOPHER MARLOWE (1564–93)

Letter to André Billy. 9 April 1915

Gunner/Driver One (front-line)
Here I am and send you greetings
No no you're not seeing things
My Sector's number fifty-nine

I hear the whistle _of
the   the bird
beautiful bird of p^r^e^y

I see^{far} ^{away}
the _{cathedral}

```
O        D
H        E
M        A
Y   A    R
N D R E
B I L L Y
```

GUILLAUME APOLLINAIRE (1880–1918)

translated by OLIVER BERNARD

Child

Your clear eye is the one absolutely beautiful thing.
I want to fill it with colour and ducks,
The zoo of the new

Whose names you meditate –
April snowdrop, Indian pipe,
Little

Stalk without wrinkle,
Pool in which images
Should be grand and classical

Not this troublous
Wringing of hands, this dark
Ceiling without a star.

SYLVIA PLATH (1932–63)

A song for England

An' a so de rain a-fall
An' a so de snow a-rain

An' a so de fog a-fall
An' a so de sun a-fail

An' a so de seasons mix
An' a so de bag-o'-tricks

But a so me understan'
De misery o' de Englishman.

ANDREW SALKEY (1928–95)

Letters from Yorkshire

In February, digging his garden, planting potatoes,
he saw the first lapwings return and came
indoors to write to me, his knuckles singing

as they reddened in the warmth.
It's not romance, simply how things are.
You out there, in the cold, seeing the seasons

turning, me with my heartful of headlines
feeding words onto a blank screen.
Is your life more real because you dig and sow?

You wouldn't say so, breaking ice on a waterbutt,
clearing a path through snow. Still, it's you
who sends me word of that other world

pouring air and light into an envelope. So that
at night, watching the same news in different houses,
our souls tap out messages across the icy miles.

MAURA DOOLEY (b. 1957)

The Bonnie Broukit Bairn

Mars is braw in crammasy,
Venus in a green silk goun,
The auld mune shak's her gowden feathers,
Their starry talk's a wheen o' blethers,
Nane for thee a thochtie sparin',
Earth, thou bonnie broukit bairn!
— *But greet, an' in your tears ye'll drown*
The haill clanjamfrie!

HUGH MacDIARMID (CHRISTOPHER MURRAY GRIEVE)
(1892–1978)

braw: fine

crammasy: crimson

a wheen o' blethers: a pack of nonsense

broukit: neglected

greet: weep

the haill clanjamfrie: the whole caboodle

'Music, when soft voices die'   Shelley's draft, extensively revised.
Bodleian Library MS Shelley adds. e.8, p.154 rev. By permission of The
Bodleian Library, University of Oxford.

To Emilia V –

Music, when soft voices die,
Vibrates in the memory –
Odours, when sweet violets sicken,
Live within the sense they quicken.

Rose leaves, when the rose is dead,
Are heaped for the beloved's bed –
And so thy thoughts, when thou art gone,
Love itself shall slumber on . . .

PERCY BYSSHE SHELLEY (1792–1822)

Concerto for Double Bass

He is a drunk leaning companionably
Around a lamp post or doing up
With intermittent concentration
Another drunk's coat.

He is a polite but devoted Valentino,
Cheek to cheek, forgetting the next step.
He is feeling the pulse of the fat lady
Or cutting her in half.

But close your eyes and it is sunset
At the edge of the world. It is the language
Of dolphins, the growth of tree-roots,
The heart-beat slowing down.

JOHN FULLER (b. 1937)

Words, Wide Night

Somewhere on the other side of this wide night
and the distance between us, I am thinking of you.
The room is turning slowly away from the moon.

This is pleasurable. Or shall I cross that out and say
it is sad? In one of the tenses I singing
an impossible song of desire that you cannot hear.

La lala la. See? I close my eyes and imagine
the dark hills I would have to cross
to reach you. For I am in love with you and this

is what it is like or what it is like in words.

CAROL ANN DUFFY (b. 1955)

The Lobster Quadrille

'Will you walk a little faster?' said a whiting to a snail,
'There's a porpoise close behind us, and he's treading on my tail.
See how eagerly the lobsters and the turtles all advance!
They are waiting on the shingle – will you come and join the dance?
   Will you, won't you, will you, won't you, will you join the dance?
   Will you, won't you, will you, won't you, won't you join the dance?

'You can really have no notion how delightful it will be
When they take us up and throw us, with the lobsters, out to sea!'
But the snail replied 'Too far, too far!', and gave a look askance –
Said he thanked the whiting kindly, but he would not join the dance.
   Would not, could not, would not, could not, would not join the dance.
   Would not, could not, would not, could not, could not join the dance.

'What matters it how far we go?' his scaly friend replied.
'There is another shore, you know, upon the other side.
The further off from England the nearer is to France –
Then turn not pale, beloved snail, but come and join the dance.
   Will you, won't you, will you, won't you, will you join the dance?
   Will you, won't you, will you, won't you, won't you join the dance?'

LEWIS CARROLL (1832–98)

The Lobster Quadrille   Illustration by John Tenniel.

'I shall say what inordinate love is'

I shall say what inordinate love is:
The furiosity and wodness of mind,
An instinguible burning, faulting bliss,
A great hunger, insatiate to find,
A dulcet ill, an evil sweetness blind,
A right wonderful sugared sweet error,
Without labour rest, contrary to kind,
Or without quiet, to have huge labour.

ANON. (15th century)

wodness: frenzy

Inordinate love   The only known source of this English version of a well-known Latin original. Thott 110, 4to., f. 163a. By permission of The Copenhagen Royal Library.

A red red Rose

O my Luve 's like a red, red rose,
   That's newly sprung in June;
O my Luve 's like the melodie
   That's sweetly play'd in tune.

As fair art thou, my bonnie lass,
   So deep in luve am I;
And I will love thee still, my Dear,
   Till a' the seas gang dry.

Till a' the seas gang dry, my Dear,
   And the rocks melt wi' the sun:
I will love thee still, my Dear,
   While the sands o' life shall run.

And fare thee weel, my only Luve!
   And fare thee weel, a while!
And I will come again, my Luve,
   Tho' it were ten thousand mile!

ROBERT BURNS (1759–96)

The Very Leaves of the Acacia-Tree are London

The very leaves of the acacia-tree are London;
London tap-water fills out the fuschia buds in the back garden
Blackbirds pull London worms out of the sour soil,
The woodlice, centipedes, eat London, the wasps even.
London air through stomata of myriad leaves
And million lungs of London breathes.
Chlorophyll and haemoglobin do what life can
To purify, to return this great explosion
To sanity of leaf and wing.
Gradual and gentle the growth of London Pride,
And sparrows are free of all the time in the world:
Less than a window-pane between.

KATHLEEN RAINE (b. 1908)

One Art

The art of losing isn't hard to master;
so many things seem filled with the intent
to be lost that their loss is no disaster.

Lose something every day. Accept the fluster
of lost door keys, the hour badly spent.
The art of losing isn't hard to master.

Then practice losing farther, losing faster:
places, and names, and where it was you meant
to travel. None of these will bring disaster.

I lost my mother's watch. And look! my last, or
next-to-last, of three loved houses went.
The art of losing isn't hard to master.

I lost two cities, lovely ones. And, vaster,
some realms I owned, two rivers, a continent.
I miss them, but it wasn't a disaster.

— Even losing you (the joking voice, a gesture
I love) I shan't have lied. It's evident
the art of losing's not too hard to master
though it may look like (*Write* it!) like disaster.

ELIZABETH BISHOP (1911–79)

To Someone Who Insisted I Look Up Someone

I rang them up while touring Timbuctoo,
Those bosom chums to whom you're known as *'Who?'*

X. J. KENNEDY (b. 1929)

Two Fragments

Love holds me captive again
and I tremble with bittersweet longing

As a gale on the mountainside bends the oak tree
I am rocked by my love

SAPPHO (fl. 600 BC)

translated by CICELY HERBERT

I Am

I am – yet what I am none cares or knows,
My friends forsake me like a memory lost;
I am the self-consumer of my woes,
They rise and vanish in oblivious host
Like shades in love and death's oblivion lost,
And yet I am – and live, with shadows tossed

Into the nothingness of scorn and noise,
Into the living sea of waking dreams,
Where there is neither sense of life nor joys,
But the vast shipwreck of my life's esteems;
And e'en the dearest, that I loved the best,
Are strange – nay, rather stranger than the rest.

I long for scenes where man has never trod,
A place where woman never smiled or wept,
There to abide with my creator, God,
And sleep as I in childhood sweetly slept,
Untroubling and untroubled where I lie;
The grass below – above the vaulted sky.

JOHN CLARE (1793–1864)

150

Dream Boogie

Good morning, daddy!
Ain't you heard
The boogie-woogie rumble
Of a dream deferred?

Listen closely:
You'll hear their feet
Beating out and beating out a —

> *You think*
> *It's a happy beat?*

Listen to it closely:
Ain't you heard
something underneath
like a —

> *What did I say?*

Sure,
I'm happy!
Take it away!

> *Hey, pop!*
> *Re-bop!*
> *Mop!*

> *Y—e—a—h!*

LANGSTON HUGHES (1902–67)

The Unpredicted

The goddess Fortune be praised (on her toothed wheel
I have been mincemeat these several years)
Last night, for a whole night, the unpredictable
Lay in my arms, in a tender and unquiet rest –
(I perceived the irrelevance of my former tears) –
Lay, and at dawn departed. I rose and walked the streets
Where a whitsuntide wind blew fresh, and blackbirds
Incontestably sang, and the people were beautiful.

JOHN HEATH-STUBBS (b. 1918)

The Emigrant Irish

Like oil lamps we put them out the back,

of our houses, of our minds. We had lights
better than, newer than and then

a time came, this time and now
we need them. Their dread, makeshift example.

They would have thrived on our necessities.
What they survived we could not even live.
By their lights now it is time to
imagine how they stood there, what they stood with,
that their possessions may become our power.

Cardboard. Iron. Their hardships parcelled in them.
Patience. Fortitude. Long-suffering
in the bruise-coloured dusk of the New World.

And all the old songs. And nothing to lose.

EAVAN BOLAND (b. 1944)

from The Garden

What wondrous life in this I lead!
Ripe apples drop about my head;
The luscious clusters of the vine
Upon my mouth do crush their wine;
The nectarine, and curious peach,
Into my hands themselves do reach;
Stumbling on melons, as I pass,
Ensnared with flowers, I fall on grass.

Meanwhile the mind, from pleasure less,
Withdraws into its happiness:
The mind, that ocean where each kind
Does straight its own resemblance find;
Yet it creates, transcending these,
Far other worlds, and other seas;
Annihilating all that's made
To a green thought in a green shade.

ANDREW MARVELL (1621–78)

The Flaw in Paganism

Drink and dance and laugh and lie,
  Love, the reeling midnight through,
For tomorrow we shall die!
  (But, alas, we never do.)

DOROTHY PARKER (1893–1967)

The Algonquin Round Table   Dorothy Parker (lower left) surrounded by
Robert Benchley, Alfred Lunt and Lynn Fontanne, Frank Crowninshield,
Alexander Woollcott, Heywood Broun, Marc Connelly, Frank Case, Franklin
P. Adams, Edna Ferber, George Kaufman and Robert Sherwood. Illustration
by Al Hirschfeld.

Anthem for Doomed Youth

What passing-bells for these who die as cattle?
   – Only the monstrous anger of the guns.
   Only the stuttering rifles' rapid rattle
Can patter out their hasty orisons.
No mockeries now for them; no prayers nor bells;
   Nor any voice of mourning save the choirs, –
The shrill demented choirs of wailing shells;
   And bugles calling for them from sad shires.

What candles may be held to speed them all?
   Not in the hands of boys, but in their eyes
Shall shine the holy glimmers of goodbyes.
   The pallor of girls' brows shall be their pall;
Their flowers the tenderness of patient minds,
And each slow dusk a drawing-down of blinds.

WILFRED OWEN (1893–1918)

What passing-bells for these who die as cattle?
    – Only the monstrous anger of the guns.
    Only the stuttering rifles' rapid rattle
Can patter out their hasty orisons.
No *music for all them, nor* mockeries for them from prayers *nor* or bells
    Nor any voice of mourning save the choirs,
The shrill *ented* demented *disconsolate* choirs of wailing shells;
    And bugles calling sad across the *for them from sad* shires.

What candles may be held to speed them all?
    Not in the hands of boys, but in their eyes
Shall shine the holy glimmers of goodbyes.
And The pallor of girl's brows shall be their pall;
Their flowers the tenderness of *silent* minds,
And each slow dusk a drawing-down of blinds.

Anthem for Doomed Youth   The pencilled corrections are by Siegfried
Sassoon, Owen's friend and fellow poet. BL Add. MS 43720, f.17.
By permission of The British Library Board.

A Picture*

for Tiantian's fifth birthday

Morning arrives in a sleeveless dress
apples tumble all over the earth
my daughter is drawing a picture
how vast is a five-year-old sky
your name has two windows
one opens towards a sun with no clock-hands
the other opens towards your father
who has become a hedgehog in exile
taking with him a few unintelligible characters
and a bright red apple
he has left your painting
how vast is a five-year-old sky

BEI DAO (b. 1949)
translated by BONNIE S. McDOUGALL
and CHEN MAIPING

*Tiantian, the nickname given to the poet's daughter, is written with two characters which look like a pair of windows. The same character also forms a part of the character for the word 'picture'.

A Picture   The first two lines of the original poem. Calligraphy by Yukki Yaura, © Yukki Yaura 1993 by permission of the artist.

Idyll

Not knowing even that we're on the way,
Until suddenly we're there. How shall we know?

There will be blackbirds, in a late March evening,
Blur of woodsmoke, whisky in grand glasses,

A poem of yours, waiting to be read; and one of mine;
A reflective bitch, a cat materialised

On a knee. All fears of present and future
Will be over, all guilts forgiven.

Maybe, heaven. Or maybe
We can get so far in this world. I'll believe we can.

U. A. FANTHORPE (b. 1929)

17 *Windsor Castle* **Adrian Allinson** 1934

18 *'Where tides of grass break into foam of flowers'* **John Farleigh** 1937

19 *'Strong blossoms with perfume of manhood'* **John Farleigh** 1937

20 *Hampton Court* **Adrian Allinson** 1934

'Gray goose and gander'

Gray goose and gander,
   Waft your wings together,
And carry the good king's daughter
   Over the one strand river.

ANON. (date unknown)

Sonnet: On His Blindness

When I consider how my light is spent,
   Ere half my days, in this dark world and wide,
   And that one talent which is death to hide,
   Lodged with me useless, though my soul more bent
To serve therewith my maker, and present
   My true account, lest he returning chide,
   Doth God exact day-labour, light denied?
   I fondly ask; but Patience to prevent
That murmur, soon replies, God doth not need
   Either man's work or his own gifts, who best
   Bear his mild yoke, they serve him best, his state
Is kingly. Thousands at his bidding speed
   And post o'er land and ocean without rest:
   They also serve who only stand and wait.

JOHN MILTON (1608–74)

He wishes for the Cloths of Heaven

Had I the heavens' embroidered cloths,
Enwrought with golden and silver light,
The blue and the dim and the dark cloths
Of night and light and the half-light,
I would spread the cloths under your feet:
But I, being poor, have only my dreams;
I have spread my dreams under your feet;
Tread softly because you tread on my dreams.

W. B. YEATS (1865–1939)

Late Summer Fires

The paddocks shave black
with a foam of smoke that stays,
welling out of red-black wounds.

In the white of a drought
this happens. The hardcourt game.
Logs that fume are mostly cattle,

inverted, stubby. Tree stumps are kilns.
Walloped, wiped, hand-pumped,
even this day rolls over, slowly.

At dusk, a family drives sheep
out through the yellow
of the Aboriginal flag.

LES MURRAY (b. 1938)

Love in a Bathtub

Years later we'll remember the bathtub,
the position
            of the taps
the water, slippery
as if a bucketful
            of eels had joined us . . .
we'll be old, our children grown up
but we'll remember the water
                        sloshing out
the useless soap,
the mountain of wet towels.
'Remember the bathtub in Belfast?'
we'll prod each other –

SUJATA BHATT (b. 1956)

The Twa Corbies

As I was walking all alane,
I heard twa corbies making a mane;
The tane unto the tither say,
'Whar sall we gang and dine the day?'

'In behint yon auld fail dyke,
I wot there lies a new-slain knight;
And naebody kens that he lies there,
But his hawk, his hound, and lady fair.

'His hound is to the hunting gane,
His hawk to fetch the wild-fowl hame,
His lady's ta'en another mate,
Sae we may mak our dinner sweet.

'Ye'll sit on his white hause-bane,
And I'll pike out his bonnie blue een:
Wi' ae lock o' his gowden hair
We'll theek our nest when it grows bare.

'Mony a one for him makes mane,
But nane sall ken whar he is gane;
O'er his white banes, when they are bare,
The wind sall blaw for evermair.'

ANON. (before 1800)

corbie: raven   *mane:* moan   *hause-bane:* neck-bone

The Great Frost

O roving Muse, recall that wondrous year,
When winter reigned in bleak Britannia's air;
When hoary Thames, with frosted osiers crowned,
Was three long moons in icy fetters bound.
The waterman, forlorn along the shore,
Pensive reclines upon his useless oar,
Sees harnessed steeds desert the stony town,
And wander roads unstable, not their own;
Wheels o'er the hardened waters smoothly glide,
And rase with whitened tracks the slippery tide.
Here the fat cook piles high the blazing fire,
And scarce the spit can turn the steer entire.
Booths sudden hide the Thames, long streets appear,
And numerous games proclaim the crowded fair.

from TRIVIA,
OR THE ART OF WALKING THE STREETS OF LONDON

JOHN GAY (1685–1732)

If I Could Tell You

Time will say nothing but I told you so,
Time only knows the price we have to pay;
If I could tell you I would let you know.

If we should weep when clowns put on their show,
If we should stumble when musicians play,
Time will say nothing but I told you so.

There are no fortunes to be told, although,
Because I love you more than I can say,
If I could tell you I would let you know.

The winds must come from somewhere when they blow,
There must be reasons why the leaves decay;
Time will say nothing but I told you so.

Perhaps the roses really want to grow,
The vision seriously intends to stay;
If I could tell you I would let you know.

Suppose the lions all get up and go,
And all the brooks and soldiers run away;
Will Time say nothing but I told you so?
If I could tell you I would let you know.

W.H. AUDEN (1907–73)

Spacetime

When I grow up and you get small,
then –

(In Kaluza's theory the fifth dimension
is represented as a circle
associated with every point
in spacetime)

– then when I die, I'll never be alive again?
                Never.
Never never?
                Never never.
Yes, but never never never?
                No . . . not never never never,
                just never never.

So we made
a small family contribution
to the quantum problem of eleven-dimensional
    supergravity.

MIROSLAV HOLUB (b. 1923)

translated by DAVID YOUNG *and* DANA HÁBOVÁ

Sun a-shine, rain a-fall

Sun a-shine an' rain a-fall,
The Devil an' him wife cyan 'gree at all,
The two o' them want one fish-head,
The Devil call him wife bonehead,
She hiss her teeth, call him cock-eye,
Greedy, worthless an' workshy,
While them busy callin' name,
The puss walk in, sey is a shame
To see a nice fish go to was'e,
Lef' with a big grin pon him face.

VALERIE BLOOM (b. 1956)

Sun a-shine, rain a-fall   Illustration by Michael Charlton.

Sonnet 18

Shall I compare thee to a summer's day?
Thou art more lovely and more temperate:
Rough winds do shake the darling buds of May,
And summer's lease hath all too short a date:
Sometime too hot the eye of heaven shines,
And often is his gold complexion dimmed;
And every fair from fair sometime declines,
By chance, or nature's changing course, untrimmed;
But thy eternal summer shall not fade,
Nor lose possession of that fair thou owest,
Nor shall death brag thou wander'st in his shade,
When in eternal lines to time thou growest;
    So long as men can breathe, or eyes can see,
    So long lives this, and this gives life to thee.

WILLIAM SHAKESPEARE (1564–1616)

A True and Faithful Inventory
of the Goods *belonging* to Dr. Swift, Vicar of Lara Cor;

upon lending his House to the Bishop of Meath,
until his own was built

An Oaken, broken, Elbow-Chair;
A Cawdle-Cup, without an Ear;
A batter'd, shatter'd Ash Bedstead;
A Box of Deal, without a Lid;
A Pair of Tongs, but out of Joint;
A Back-Sword Poker, without Point;
A Pot that's crack'd across, around,
With an old knotted Garter bound;
An iron lock, without a Key;
A Wig, with hanging, quite grown grey;
A Curtain worn to Half a Stripe;
A Pair of Bellows, without Pipe;
A Dish, which might good Meat afford once;
An *Ovid*, and an old *Concordance*;
A Bottle Bottom, Wooden Platter,
One is for Meal, and one for Water:
There likewise is a Copper Skillet,
Which runs as fast out as you fill it;
A Candlestick, Snuff dish, and Save-all,
And thus his Household Goods you have all.
These, to your Lordship, as a Friend,
Till you have built, I freely lend:
They'll save your Lordship for a Shift;
Why not, as well as Doctor *Swift?*

THOMAS SHERIDAN (1687–1738)

Where Go the Boats?

Dark brown is the river,
    Golden is the sand.
It flows along for ever,
    With trees on either hand.

Green leaves a-floating,
    Castles of the foam,
Boats of mine a-boating –
    Where will all come home?

On goes the river
    And out past the mill,
Away down the valley,
    Away down the hill.

Away down the river,
    A hundred miles or more,
Other little children
    Shall bring my boats ashore.

ROBERT LOUIS STEVENSON (1850–94)

Where Go the Boats? Illustrations by A.H. Watson from
A Child's Garden of Verses, Collins (1946)

Thanks Forever

Look at those empty ships
floating north
between south-running ice
like big tulips
in the Narrows
under the Verrazano
toward the city harbor.
I'm parked here,
out of work all year.
No hurry now
and sleep badly.
But I'm self-employed.
My new job's
to wave them in.
Hello freighter,
hello tanker.
Welcome, welcome,
to New York.

MILTON KESSLER (b. 1930)

Swineherd

When all this is over, said the swineherd,
I mean to retire, where
Nobody will have heard about my special skills
And conversation is mainly about the weather.

I intend to learn how to make coffee, at least as well
As the Portuguese lay-sister in the kitchen
And polish the brass fenders every day.
I want to lie awake at night
Listening to cream crawling to the top of the jug
And the water lying soft in the cistern.

I want to see an orchard where the trees grow in straight lines
And the yellow fox finds shelter between the navy-blue trunks,
Where it gets dark early in summer
And the apple-blossom is allowed to wither on the bough.

EILÉAN NÍ CHUILLEANÁIN (b. 1942)

'The world is too much with us'

The world is too much with us; late and soon,
Getting and spending, we lay waste our powers:
Little we see in nature that is ours;
We have given our hearts away, a sordid boon!
This Sea that bares her bosom to the moon;
The Winds that will be howling at all hours
And are up-gathered now like sleeping flowers;
For this, for every thing, we are out of tune;
It moves us not. Great God! I'd rather be
A Pagan suckled in a creed outworn;
So might I, standing on this pleasant lea,
Have glimpses that would make me less forlorn;
Have sight of Proteus coming from the sea;
Or hear old Triton blow his wreathed horn.

WILLIAM WORDSWORTH (1770–1850)

The world is too much with us; late and soon
Getting and spending we lay waste our powers
Little we see in nature that is ours;
We have given our hearts away, a sordid boon.
This sea that bares her bosom to the moon
The winds that will be howling at all hours,
And are upgather'd now like sleeping flowers,
For this, for every thing we are out of tune:
It moves us not. Great God! I'd rather be
A Pagan suckled in a creed outworn
So might I, standing on this pleasant lea
Have glimpses that would make me less
Have sight of Proteus coming from the sea
Or hear old Triton blow his wreathed horn.

From DC MS 44, a homemade notebook of Wordsworth's then
unpublished work, copied by his sister Dorothy and his wife Mary, for
Coleridge to take with him on a visit to Malta in 1804. The hand on this
poem is Dorothy Wordsworth's; the overlaid word 'hearts' is written by
William Wordsworth. DC MS 44 is one of the most important sources of
Wordsworth's early work. Reprinted by permission of The Wordsworth
Trust.

A Birthday

My heart is like a singing bird
    Whose nest is in a watered shoot;
My heart is like an apple-tree
    Whose boughs are bent with thick-set fruit;
My heart is like a rainbow shell
    That paddles in a halcyon sea;
My heart is gladder than all these
    Because my love is come to me.

Raise me a dais of silk and down;
    Hang it with vair and purple dyes;
Carve it in doves and pomegranates,
    And peacocks with a hundred eyes;
Work it in gold and silver grapes,
    In leaves and silver fleurs-de-lys;
Because the birthday of my life
    Is come, my love is come to me.

CHRISTINA ROSSETTI (1830–94)

Disillusionment of Ten O'Clock

The houses are haunted
By white night-gowns.
None are green,
Or purple with green rings,
Or green with yellow rings,
Or yellow with blue rings.
None of them are strange,
With socks of lace
And beaded ceintures.
People are not going
To dream of baboons and periwinkles.
Only, here and there, an old sailor,
Drunk and asleep in his boots,
Catches tigers
In red weather.

WALLACE STEVENS (1879–1955)

The Boundary Commission

You remember that village where the border ran
Down the middle of the street,
With the butcher and baker in different states?
Today he remarked how a shower of rain

Had stopped so cleanly across Golightly's lane
It might have been a wall of glass
That had toppled over. He stood there, for ages,
To wonder which side, if any, he should be on.

PAUL MULDOON (b. 1951)

Arrival 1946

The boat docked in at Liverpool.
From the train Tariq stared
at an unbroken line of washing
from the North West to Euston.

These are strange people, he thought –
an Empire, and all this washing,
the underwear, the Englishman's garden.
It was Monday, and very sharp.

MONIZA ALVI (b. 1954)

'Now winter nights enlarge'

Now winter nights enlarge
   The number of their hours,
And clouds their storms discharge
   Upon the airy towers.
Let now the chimneys blaze,
   And cups o'erflow with wine:
Let well-tun'd words amaze
   With harmony divine.
Now yellow waxen lights
   Shall wait on honey Love,
While youthful Revels, Masks, and Courtly sights,
   Sleep's leaden spells remove.

This time doth well dispense
   With lovers' long discourse;
Much speech hath some defence,
   Though beauty no remorse.
All do not all things well;
   Some measures comely tread;
Some knotted Riddles tell;
   Some Poems smoothly read.
The Summer hath his joys,
   And Winter his delights;
Though Love and all his pleasures are but toys.
   They shorten tedious nights.

THOMAS CAMPION (1567–1620)

'Let my shadow disappear into yours'

Låt min skugga försvinna i din.
Låt mig förlora mig själv
under de stora träden.
De som själva förlorar sin krona i skymningen,
överlämnar sig åt himmelen och natten.

Let my shadow disappear into yours.
Let me lose myself
under the tall trees,
that themselves lose their crowns in the twilight,
surrendering themselves to the sky and the night.

PÄR LAGERKVIST (1891–1974)
translated by W. H. AUDEN *and* LEIF SJÖBERG

Do Not Go Gentle Into That Good Night

Do not go gentle into that good night,
Old age should burn and rave at close of day;
Rage, rage against the dying of the light.

Though wise men at their end know dark is right,
Because their words had forked no lightning they
Do not go gentle into that good night.

Good men, the last wave by, crying how bright
Their frail deeds might have danced in a green bay,
Rage, rage against the dying of the light.

Wild men who caught and sang the sun in flight,
And learn, too late, they grieved it on its way,
Do not go gentle into that good night.

Grave men, near death, who see with blinding sight
Blind eyes could blaze like meteors and be gay,
Rage, rage against the dying of the light.

And you, my father, there on the sad height,
Curse, bless, me now with your fierce tears, I pray.
Do not go gentle into that good night.
Rage, rage against the dying of the light.

DYLAN THOMAS (1914–53)

Look at all those monkeys

Look at all those monkeys
Jumping in their cage.
Why don't they all go out to work
And earn a decent wage?

> *How can you say such silly things,*
> *And you a son of mine?*
> *Imagine monkeys travelling on*
> *The Morden–Edgware line!*

But what about the Pekinese!
They have an allocation.
'Don't travel during Peke hour',
It says on every station.

> *My Gosh, you're right, my clever boy,*
> *I never thought of that!*
> And so they left the monkey house,
> While an elephant raised his hat.

SPIKE MILLIGAN (b. 1918)

Mysteries

At night, I do not know who I am
when I dream, when I am sleeping.

Awakened, I hold my breath and listen:
a thumbnail scratches the other side of the wall.

At midday, I enter a sunlit room
to observe the lamplight on for no reason.

I should know by now that few octaves can be heard,
that a vision dies from being too long stared at;

that the whole of recorded history even
is but a little gossip in a great silence;

that a magnesium flash cannot illumine,
for one single moment, the invisible.

I do not complain. I start with the visible
and am startled by the visible.

DANNIE ABSE (b. 1923)

Rooms

Though I love this travelling life and yearn
like ships docked, I long
for rooms to open with my bare hands,
and there discover the wonderful, say
a ship's prow rearing, and a ladder
of rope thrown down.
Though young, I'm weary:
I'm all rooms at present, all doors
fastened against me;
but once admitted start craving
and swell for a fine, listing ocean-going prow
no man in creation can build me.

KATHLEEN JAMIE (b. 1962)

The Good Morrow

I wonder, by my troth, what thou and I
Did, till we loved; were we not weaned till then,
But sucked on country pleasures, childishly?
Or snorted we in the Seven Sleepers' den?
'Twas so; but this, all pleasures fancies be.
If ever any beauty I did see,
Which I desired, and got, 'twas but a dream of thee.

And now good morrow to our waking souls,
Which watch not one another out of fear;
For love, all love of other sights controls,
And makes one little room, an everywhere.
Let sea-discoverers to new worlds have gone,
Let maps to others, worlds on worlds have shown,
Let us possess our world; each hath one, and is one.

My face in thine eye, thine in mine appears,
And true plain hearts do in the faces rest;
Where can we find two better hemispheres,
Without sharp North, without declining West?
Whatever dies, was not mixed equally;
If our two loves be one; or thou and I
Love so alike that none do slacken, none can die.

JOHN DONNE (1572–1631)

Adlestrop

Yes. I remember Adlestrop –
The name, because one afternoon
Of heat the express-train drew up there
Unwontedly. It was late June.

The steam hissed. Someone cleared his throat.
No one left and no one came
On the bare platform. What I saw
Was Adlestrop – only the name

And willows, willow-herb, and grass,
And meadowsweet, and haycocks dry,
No whit less still and lonely fair
Than the high cloudlets in the sky.

And for that minute a blackbird sang
Close by, and round him, mistier,
Farther and farther, all the birds
Of Oxfordshire and Gloucestershire.

EDWARD THOMAS (1878–1917)

from Requiem

The hour of remembrance has drawn close again.
I see you, hear you, feel you:

the one they could hardly get to the window,
the one who no longer walks on this earth,

the one who shook her beautiful head,
and said: 'Coming here is like coming home.'

I would like to name them all but they took away
the list and there's no way of finding them.

For them I have woven a wide shroud
from the humble words I heard among them.

I remember them always, everywhere,
I will never forget them, whatever comes.

ANNA AKHMATOVA (1889–1966)
translated by RICHARD McKANE

The Exiles

translated from the author's own Gaelic

The many ships that left our country
with white wings for Canada.
They are like handkerchiefs in our memories
and the brine like tears
and in their masts sailors singing
like birds on branches.
That sea of May running in such blue,
a moon at night, a sun at daytime,
and the moon like a yellow fruit,
like a plate on a wall
to which they raise their hands
like a silver magnet
with piercing rays
streaming into the heart.

IAIN CRICHTON SMITH (b. 1928)

Moonwise

(for my children, all)

sometimes
you know
the moon
is not such a perfect
circle

and the master Painter
makes a passing
brush touch
with a cloud

don't worry
we've passed
the dark side

all you children
rest easy now

we are born

moonwise

JEAN 'BINTA' BREEZE (b. 1956)

. . . all your quaint enameld eyes
That on the green terf suck the honied showres
And purple all the ground with vernal flowres.

Milton : Lycidas

 OUT AND ABOUT BY LONDON TRANSPORT

21 *Out and About by London Transport* **John Farleigh** 1958

22 *Country Walks – Spring ('For winter's rains and ruins are over')* **Paul Millichip** 1957

'Where the thistle lifts a purple crown
Six feet out of the turf,
And the harebell shakes on the windy hill...' FRANCIS THOMPSON

London Transport's Country Walks books are your sure guide to miles of rambles through the green pleasantness of London's country. They contain detailed path routes, sketch maps and details of how to get there and back, and cost 2/6 each. The new series 3 (with Ordnance Survey maps) cost 3/6. Buy them at Underground ticket offices and book stalls, at the Travel Enquiry Offices at Piccadilly Circus and St. James's Park stations, or from the Publicity Officer, 55 Broadway, S.W.1

Make the most of your public transport

23 *Country Walks – Summer ('Where the thistle lifts a purple crown')* **Robert Tavener** 1958

'The height and spread of frontage shining sheer
The quiring signs, the rejoicing roofs and spires –
'Tis El Dorado – El Dorado plain
The Golden City . . .' Can you identify this quotation?

Two TWIN ROVER tickets will be sent to each of the first ten applicants to name correctly the author and the poem from which it is taken. Postcards please to the Publicity Officer, 55 Broadway, S.W.1.

24 *London Rovers ('The height and spread of frontage shining sheer')* **Peter Roberson** 1958

'My true love hath my heart and I have his'

My true love hath my heart and I have his,
By just exchange one for the other given.
I hold his dear, and mine he cannot miss,
There never was a better bargain driven.
   My true love hath my heart and I have his.

His heart in me keeps me and him in one,
My heart in him his thoughts and senses guides:
He loves my heart, for once it was his own,
I cherish his because in me it bides.
   My true love hath my heart, and I have his.

SIR PHILIP SIDNEY (1554–86)

Acquainted with the Night

I have been one acquainted with the night.
I have walked out in rain – and back in rain.
I have outwalked the furthest city light.

I have looked down the saddest city lane.
I have passed by the watchman on his beat
And dropped my eyes, unwilling to explain.

I have stood still and stopped the sound of feet
When far away an interrupted cry
Came over houses from another street,

But not to call me back or say good-by;
And further still at an unearthly height
One luminary clock against the sky

Proclaimed the time was neither wrong nor right.
I have been one acquainted with the night.

ROBERT FROST (1874–1963)

from Summoned by Bells

Great was my joy with London at my feet –
All London mine, five shillings in my hand
And not expected back till after tea!
Great was our joy, Ronald Hughes Wright's and mine,
To travel by the Underground all day
Between the rush hours, so that very soon
There was no station, north to Finsbury Park,
To Barking eastwards, Clapham Common south,
No temporary platform in the west
Among the Actons and the Ealings, where
We had not once alighted. Metroland
Beckoned us out to lanes in beechy Bucks –
Goldschmidt and Howland (in a wooden hut
Beside the station): 'Most attractive sites
Ripe for development'; Charrington's for coal;
And not far off the neo-Tudor shops.

JOHN BETJEMAN (1906–84)

Summoned by Bells   'The Underground' by Hugh Casson, from *The Illustrated Summoned by Bells*, with paintings and sketches by Hugh Casson (John Murray 1989). By permission of the artist. © Hugh Casson 1989.

A Glass of Water

Here is a glass of water from my well.
It tastes of rock and root and earth and rain;
It is the best I have, my only spell,
And it is cold, and better than champagne.
Perhaps someone will pass this house one day
To drink, and be restored, and go his way,
Someone in dark confusion as I was
When I drank down cold water in a glass,
Drank a transparent health to keep me sane,
After the bitter mood had gone again.

MAY SARTON (1912–95)

Wind

This is the wind, the wind in a field of corn.
Great crowds are fleeing from a major disaster
Down the long valleys, the green swaying wadis,
Down through the beautiful catastrophe of wind.

Families, tribes, nations and their livestock
Have heard something, seen something. An expectation
Or a gigantic misunderstanding has swept over the hilltop
Bending the ear of the hedgerow with stories of fire and sword.

I saw a thousand years pass in two seconds.
Land was lost, languages rose and divided.
This lord went east and found safety.
His brother sought Africa and a dish of aloes.

Centuries, minutes later, one might ask
How the hilt of a sword wandered so far from the smithy.
And somewhere they will sing: 'Like chaff we were borne
In the wind.' This is the wind in a field of corn.

JAMES FENTON (b. 1949)

To My Dear and Loving Husband

If ever two were one, then surely we.
If ever man were loved by wife, then thee;
If ever wife was happy in a man,
Compare with me ye women if you can.
I prize thy love more than whole mines of gold,
Or all the riches that the East doth hold.
My love is such that rivers cannot quench,
Nor ought but love from thee give recompence.
Thy love is such I can no way repay,
The heavens reward thee manifold I pray.
Then while we live, in love let's so persever,
That when we live no more, we may live ever.

ANNE BRADSTREET (1612–72)

Chorus from a Play
(written in the year 1700)

All, all, of a piece throughout;
Thy chase had a beast in view;
Thy wars brought nothing about;
Thy lovers were all untrue.
'Tis well an old age is out,
And time to begin a new.

JOHN DRYDEN (1631–1700)

Inversnaid

This dárksome búrn, hórseback brówn,
His rollrock highroad roaring down,
In coop and in comb the fleece of his foam
Flutes and low to the lake falls home.

A windpuff-bónnet of fáwn-fróth
Turns and twindles over the broth
Of a pool so pitchblack, féll-frówning,
It rounds and rounds Despair to drowning.

Degged with dew, dappled with dew
Are the groins of the braes that the brook treads through,
Wiry heathpacks, flitches of fern,
And the beadbonny ash that sits over the burn.

What would the world be, once bereft
Of wet and of wildness? Let them be left,
O let them be left, wildness and wet;
Long live the weeds and the wilderness yet.

GERARD MANLEY HOPKINS (1844–89)

Saturday Morning

Everyone who made love the night before
was walking around with flashing red lights
on top of their heads – a white-haired old gentleman,
a red-faced schoolboy, a pregnant woman
who smiled at me from across the street
and gave a little secret shrug,
as if the flashing red light on her head
was a small price to pay for what she knew.

HUGO WILLIAMS (b. 1942)

The Undertaking

The darkness lifts, imagine, in your lifetime.
There you are – cased in clean bark you drift
through weaving rushes, fields flooded with cotton.
You are free. The river films with lilies,
shrubs appear, shoots thicken into palm. And now
all fear gives way: the light
looks after you, you feel the waves' goodwill
as arms widen over the water; Love,

the key is turned. Extend yourself –
it is the Nile, the sun is shining,
everywhere you turn is luck.

LOUISE GLÜCK (b. 1943)

His Return to London

From the dull confines of the drooping West,
To see the day spring from the pregnant East,
Ravished in spirit, I come, nay more, I fly
To thee, blest place of my nativity!
Thus, thus with hallowed foot I touch the ground,
With thousand blessings by thy fortune crowned.
O fruitful Genius! that bestowest here
An everlasting plenty, year by year.
O place! O people! Manners! framed to please
All nations, customs, kindreds, languages!
I am a free-born Roman; suffer then,
That I amongst you live a citizen.
London my home is: though by hard fate sent
Into a long and irksome banishment;
Yet since called back; henceforward let me be,
O native country, repossessed by thee!
For, rather than I'll to the West return,
I'll beg of thee first here to have mine urn.
Weak I am grown, and must in short time fall;
Give thou my sacred relics burial.

ROBERT HERRICK (1591–1674)

'I taste a liquor never brewed'

I taste a liquor never brewed –
From Tankards scooped in Pearl –
Not all the Vats upon the Rhine
Yield such an Alcohol!

Inebriate of Air – am I –
And Debauchee of Dew –
Reeling – thro endless summer days –
From inns of Molten Blue –

When "Landlords" turn the drunken Bee
Out of the Foxglove's door –
When Butterflies – renounce their "drams" –
I shall but drink the more!

Till Seraphs swing their snowy Hats –
And Saints – to windows run –
To see the little Tippler
Leaning against the – Sun –

EMILY DICKINSON (1830–86)

The Poet

Therefore he no more troubled the pool of silence.
But put on mask and cloak,
Strung a guitar
And moved among the folk.
Dancing they cried,
'Ah, how our sober islands
Are gay again, since this blind lyrical tramp
Invaded the Fair!'

Under the last dead lamp
When all the dancers and masks had gone inside
His cold stare
Returned to its true task, interrogation of silence.

GEORGE MACKAY BROWN (1921–96)

Greenwich Park

Spring's come, a little late, in the park:
a tree-rat smokes flat S's over the lawn.
A mallard has somehow forgotten something
it can't quite remember. Daffodils yawn,
prick their ears, push their muzzles out
for a kiss. Pansies spoof pensive
Priapus faces: Socrates or Verlaine.
A cock-pigeon is sexually harassing
a hen: pecking and poking and padding
behind her impertinently, bowing and mowing.
But when he's suddenly absent-minded –
can't keep even sex in his head –
she trembles, stops her gadding, doubts
and grazes his way. He remembers and pouts.

HERBERT LOMAS (b. 1924)

Apology

Humming your Nocturne on the Circle Line,
unlike the piano, running out of breath

I've been writing you out of my life
my loves (one out, one in).

I've pushed you out of the way to see
what the gaps in my life might look like,

how large they are,
how quickly I could write them in;

and not (at least till I've lost you both)
rewriting you only means

that the spaces I'm not writing in are where
I live.

MIMI KHALVATI (b. 1944)

'Under the greenwood tree'

Under the greenwood tree
Who loves to lie with me,
And turn his merry note
Unto the sweet bird's throat,
Come hither, come hither, come hither:
    Here shall he see
    No enemy
But winter and rough weather.

Who doth ambition shun
And loves to live i' th' sun,
Seeking the food he eats,
And pleased with what he gets,
Come hither, come hither, come hither:
    Here shall he see
    No enemy
But winter and rough weather.

from AS YOU LIKE IT

WILLIAM SHAKESPEARE (1564–1616)

from **Poetry**

And it was at that age . . . Poetry arrived
in search of me. I don't know, I don't know where
it came from, from winter or a river.
I don't know how or when,
no, they were not voices, they were not
words, nor silence,
but from a street I was summoned,
from the branches of night,
abruptly from the others,
among violent fires
or returning alone,
there I was without a face
and it touched me.

Y fue a esa edad . . . Llegó la poesía
a buscarme. No sé, no sé de dónde
salió, de invierno o río.
No sé cómo ni cuándo,
no, no eran voces, no eran
palabras, ni silencio,
pero desde una calle me llamaba,
desde las ramas de la noche,
de pronto entre los otros,
entre fuegos violentos
o regresando solo,
alli estaba sin rostro
y me tocaba.

PABLO NERUDA (1904–73)
translated by ALASTAIR REID

Memory of my Father

Every old man I see
Reminds me of my father
When he had fallen in love with death
One time when sheaves were gathered.

That man I saw in Gardner Street
Stumble on the kerb was one,
He stared at me half-eyed,
I might have been his son.

And I remember the musician
Faltering over his fiddle
In Bayswater, London,
He too set me the riddle.

Every old man I see
In October-coloured weather
Seems to say to me:
'I was once your father.'

PATRICK KAVANAGH (1906–67)

Secret Lives

Sometimes your dressing gown unhooks
and slides out under the garden door,
with three aces up his sleeve.

He flies in the face of next door's dog,
and backflips down the middle of the street,
opening himself and humming.

Something in pink nylon flutters at him
from a bedroom window. He twirls his cord
to beckon her outside.

They're heading for a club they know
where the dress code is relaxed midweek,
and the music is strictly soul.

SIÂN HUGHES

Potosí

The moon falls
like a metaphysician
on the silver city

so distressed a metal –
even the horses shod with silver
in the freezing streets

wagons, blue with graffiti
under the spoil-tips,
and at first light

mountain foxes,
red as cinnabar,
moving against the flow

between the silver-bearing lodes,
the upland snow.

PAULINE STAINER

The Lesson (an anti-pastoral)

The small schoolgirl
　on her way down
　　grey Portugal Lane
　　late for class
who brushes a careless
　hand against
　　the one green
　　　nettle that had to sprout
　　from yards of concrete
can't believe
　there's no dock leaf
　　　to cancel
　　　it out.

TRACY RYAN

NOTES TO THE POEMS

page 25 **Up in the Morning Early**   'The chorus of this song is old; the two stanzas are mine' (Burns's note).

33 **The Trees**   Philip Larkin was on the Compton Poetry Fund committee when it approved a grant which enabled us to pay for the first year of advertising spaces on the Underground. He took a special interest in the project and wrote to us with useful suggestions: 'I have always liked the Wayside Pulpit placards (''Don't Put Your Wishbone Where Your Backbone Ought To Be''), and think it might be equally inspiring to be able to read on a tube journey poems that served as a reminder that the world of the imagination existed . . . What level of appreciation are you aiming at? Somerset Maugham, in his play-writing days, said that if you saw the audiences' taste in terms of the alphabet, it was best to aim at letter O. I don't think it would hurt to remind people of poems they already know; not everyone will know them.' Shortly before his death, he wrote to us again: 'I am glad your project is being favourably regarded; it makes me wonder whether I shall ever actually see one of the poems in the proposed location.' Sadly, he died before the first set of poems was posted.

35 **The Sick Rose**   William Blake, known in his own day as an engraver rather than a poet, published his *Songs of Innocence* and *Songs of Experience* in hand-engraved, hand-coloured editions of his own design ('illuminated printing'). This meant, in effect, that the poems remained virtually unknown until Blake was rediscovered as a great visionary poet in the 1860s. Both 'The Sick Rose' and 'The Tyger' were published in *Songs of Experience* (1794).

37 **At Lord's**   Cricket's laureate is Francis Thompson, whose 'At Lord's' evokes the image of an exiled Lancastrian watching a match at Lord's cricket ground but seeing in his mind's eye a game played elsewhere, many years before. The poem is a reduced version of a longer poem which mentions, as well as the Lancashire batsmen Hornby and

Barlow, Gloucestershire's 'resistless' Grace brothers. When the poster appeared on the Tube, the former cricketer Mike Selvey reprinted it in full in his *Guardian* Cricket Diary ('No, this isn't the arts page – just a bit of our cultural heritage for a change') and we were inundated with requests for the poem, mostly from Lancashire.

41 **Composed Upon Westminster Bridge** 'Written on the roof of a coach, on my way to France' (Wordsworth's note). With Wordsworth's dating of the poem in mind, we arranged a 'workshop' on Westminster Bridge at dawn on 3 September 1986. We advertised in the London listings magazines and to our amazement between twenty and thirty people turned up, including a visiting American professor and the poet Wendy Cope. At dawn (twelve minutes past six, BST) we read the poem aloud. Then we settled down to watch the sun rise and write some poems of our own. Aware that the Thames crosses England from west to east, we gazed downstream, waiting to see the sun. We might have waited a very long time, as on this stretch the Thames runs due north (towards Islington, York and the Arctic circle). In any case, it was an overcast morning. When the sun suddenly gleamed through, apparently to our south, were were mightily surprised. Once we were cold enough, we adjourned to a local coffee shop to warm up and read our poems.

When T. S. Eliot's 'Prelude' was displayed on the Tube, we held a second 'winter' workshop at dusk on Waterloo Bridge, somewhat impeded by rain and sleet.

43 **The Loch Ness Monster's Song** The author explained in conversation that the lonely monster rises from the loch and looks round for the companions of his youth – prehistoric reptiles – and, finding nobody he knows, he descends again to the depths after a brief swearing session. This was confirmed by a nine-year-old boy in a workshop, who said the monster was 'looking for a diplodocus'. When asked how he knew that, he said, 'It says so.' It does.

Some years ago, Edwin Morgan was commissioned by the Scottish Arts Council to write a series of poems for the inauguration of Glasgow's refurbished Underground system. He sent us this sample, which sent such alarm through the Strathclyde transport executive that they decided against using the poems.

The Subway Piranhas

Did anyone tell you
that in each subway train
there is one special seat
with a small hole in it
and underneath the seat
is a tank of piranha-fish
which have not been fed
for quite some time.
The fish become agitated
by the shoogling of the train
and jump up through the seat.
The resulting skeletons
of unlucky passengers
turn an honest penny
for the transport executive,
hanging far and wide
in medical schools.

44 **Living**   On learning that a poem of hers was to appear on the Underground, Denise Levertov, who was born in London but has lived mainly in the United States, wrote to us: 'I am totally thrilled at the idea of having a poem in the Tube. I spent innumerable hours in the Tube from age 12–23, and a good many before and since, too. I am in fact a sort of Tube Rat, like a "rat" of the Paris Opera – a *denizen*. Appearance in American trains and buses means little to me – but London, ah, London! – that's different.'

49 **I Am Becoming My Mother**   The title poem of a volume for which Lorna Goodison was awarded the Commonwealth Poetry Prize (Americas region) for 1986.

50 **'Tagus farewell'**   Written in June 1539 in Spain, where Wyatt was Ambassador at the court of Charles V. Wyatt had just been recalled to London by Henry VIII, and the last lines of the poem may reflect some uneasiness at the fate awaiting him at home. The Spanish and Portuguese River Tagus is famous for its gold. Brutus, a descendant of Aeneas, dreamed that he was destined to found a kingdom in Albion.

53   **Lines** *from* **Endymion**   The famous opening lines of a long poem, and the first of a number of extracts in our collection.

54   **Goodbye**   Charlie Parker was an American jazz saxophonist, possibly the greatest of them all, who died in 1955, aged thirty-four.

57   **'So we'll go no more a-roving'**   Written in a letter to Thomas Moore in which Byron admits to over-indulging in carnival festivities: 'The mumming closed with a masked ball at the Fenice, where I went, as also to most of the ridottos, etc., etc., and, though I did not dissipate much upon the whole, yet I find ''the sword wearing out the scabbard'', though I have but just turned the corner of twenty-nine.'

71   **The Coming of Grendel**   Another extract. In this passage from the Old English epic, the monster Grendel (the original inhabitant of the land) closes in on the glittering wine-hall of the colonisers, where he means to wreak terrible havoc. The translation tries to be as literal as possible, while keeping the linguistic feeling of the original, with its resounding alliteration.

73   **Sonnet from the Portuguese**   The sonnets have no Portuguese original; they were written in secret the year before the poet's marriage to Robert Browning and tell the story of their unfolding love. In a letter to Leigh Hunt, Robert Browning explained how he persuaded Elizabeth Barrett Browning to publish these intimate poems: 'I never suspected the existence of those ''Sonnets from the Portuguese'' till three years after they were written. They were shown to me in consequence of some word of mine, just as they had been suppressed through some mistaken word; it was I who would not bear that sacrifice, and thought of the subterfuge of a name.' The sequence of forty-three sonnets appears as the final work in *Poems of Elizabeth Barrett Browning* (1850), immediately preceded by 'Catarina to Camoens' – a love poem addressed by his dying mistress to the great sixteenth-century Portuguese poet. The suggestion is that 'Catarina' may have written the Sonnets as well, though this is not said explicitly – and the poems quickly became among the most celebrated love poems in the English language.

77   **Symphony in Yellow**   The sketch of Wilde was formerly attributed to Whistler, rather than to his wife Beatrice. They were friends and neighbours of Wilde's in Tite Street, Chelsea.

79   **'Sumer is icumen in'**   Robert Graves and Laura Riding comment in their paper 'On Anthologies': 'Every possible polite explanation is given in popular anthologies for *verteth* to distract attention from the poetic meaning that the buck, full of Spring grass, *farteth*, i.e. breaks wind.' Scholarly debate still rages on this question, but on balance we agree with Graves and Riding, and have emended our earlier version.

90   **Roundel** *from* **The Parliament of Fowls**   Sung by the assembled birds at the end of the St Valentine's Day festivities, when each bird has been happily paired off with its mate. 'The note,' the narrator explains, 'imaked was in France' – home of courtly love, which Chaucer's delicious poem gently parodies.

95   *from* **To the City of London**   The fourth stanza of a seven-stanza 'balade' recited during Christmas week, 1501, at a dinner held by the Lord Mayor in honour of the visiting Scottish Ambassador. Usually assumed to be the work of the Scottish poet William Dunbar, who was in London at the time.

96   **On First Looking into Chapman's Homer**   Composed during October 1816, at dawn, as Keats walked home to Southwark from Clerkenwell, where he had been visiting his former schoolteacher Charles Cowden Clarke. They had stayed up all night reading Homer in the magnificent translation of George Chapman.

00   **'I have a gentil cock'**   We have retained the old spelling of 'gentil' to suggest 'gently bred' or 'aristocratic'. Chanticleer, in Chaucer's *Nun's Priest's Tale*, is another 'gentil cock', described in similar terms:

> His coomb was redder than the fyn coral,
> And batailled as it were a castel wal;
> His byle was blak, and as the jeet it shoon,
> Lyk asure were his legges and his toon,
> His nayles whitter than the lylye flour,
> And lyk the burned gold was his colour.

(lines 39–44)

03   **Mmenson**   *mmenson:* an orchestra of seven elephant tusk horns used on state occasions to relate history; *Agades*: a town in the western

Sudan; *Sokoto*: a town in what is now northern Nigeria. (Notes by the author.)

104   **Light**   Diane Wakoski felt that the extract from 'The Hitchhikers' which originally appeared on the Underground would represent a distortion of the poem if reproduced in a book, and we were happy to substitute this complete short poem.

106   **'You took away all the oceans and all the room'**   In 1934, after he was discovered to be the author of a bitter satire on Stalin, Mandelstam was arrested and exiled for three years, first to a small town in the Urals, then to the provincial town of Voronezh, where this poem was written. He was rearrested in 1938, and died en route to a labour camp.

110   **Old English Riddle**   Suggested answer: *Bookworm*. This reminds us that bookworms have always been a genuine problem to book owners. This charming riddle is No. 47 in *The Exeter Book*, probably transcribed c. 960–70 and later owned by the first Bishop of Exeter. The riddles vary greatly in subject and style. Many are about the animal kingdom, others are about artefacts and yet others about the forces of nature – and there is a sprinkling of teasing double entendre, of a type still popular, which leads the reader to imagine two parallel solutions, one obscene, the other innocent.

118   **The Cries of London**   Two stanzas of a broadside ballad in the 'Roxburghe Ballads', a unique collection of songs and ballads printed between 1560 and 1700, collected by Robert, Earl of Oxford, and now in the British Library. The 'cries' can be heard to this day in many traditional London markets.

122   **'Ich am of Irlonde'**   Fragment of a medieval carol, written with other rhymes and doggerel in French and English on a single vellum leaf, now in the Bodleian Library, Oxford. W. B. Yeats uses the lines as a refrain for 'I am of Ireland', in *Words for Music Perhaps*:

> *'I am of Ireland,*
> *And the Holy Land of Ireland,*
> *And time runs on,' cried she.*
> *'Come out of charity,*
> *Come dance with me in Ireland.'*

126 **"The Uncertainty of the Poet"**   'The Tate Gallery yesterday announced that it had paid £1 million for a Giorgio de Chirico masterpiece, The Uncertainty of the Poet. It depicts a torso and a bunch of bananas' – *Guardian*, 2 April 1985. *With a Poet's Eye: A Tate Gallery Anthology*, for which the poem was first commissioned, presents paintings and poems side by side.

127 **'I saw a Peacock with a fiery tail'**   In his anthology *Come Hither* (1923), Walter de la Mare comments: 'So may the omission of a few commas effect a wonder in the imagination.' The first printing we were able to find was in *Westminster Drollery, Or, A Choice Collection of the Newest Songs and Poems both at Court and Theaters*, by A Person of Quality (1671). There the verse is headed: 'These following are to be understood two ways', and commas half-way through each line encourage the reader to pick up the double meaning. We have followed later editors in omitting the commas.

130 **On Himself**   The poet, who died in 1994, had been profoundly deaf since the age of seven, following an attack of scarlet fever. This poem appeared on the Underground in September 1991. A 1992 collection of David Wright's poems includes these moving lines:

An Appearance of Success

> Some verses, written when he was alive,
> A poster broadcast on the Underground;
> My life (an actor plays him) televised;
> Fame of a kind, if not recognition;
> Pleasing enough but not enough to please
> An unambitiousness at seventy-one,
> Or pierce the unawareness of the dead:
> This present I'd have loved to give to him
> To make amends,
> – My father – an appearance of success
> In his deaf difficult son;
> Something to recompense
> As may have seemed to him
> Rewardless and too long a sacrifice.

132 **The Passionate Shepherd to his Love** Because of limited space, in our Underground poster we adapted the four-stanza version published in *The Passionate Pilgrim* (1599). The six-stanza version published in *England's Helicon* (1600) has been reprinted ever since in this form, often with its companion piece, 'The Nymph's Reply to the Shepherd' by Sir Walter Raleigh:

> If all the world and love were young,
> And truth in every shepherd's tongue,
> These pretty pleasures might me move
> To live with thee and be thy love.
>
> Time drives the flocks from field to fold,
> When rivers rage and rocks grow cold,
> And Philomel becometh dumb;
> The rest complains of cares to come.
>
> The flowers do fade, and wanton fields
> To wayward winter reckoning yields;
> A honey tongue, a heart of gall,
> Is fancy's spring, but sorrow's fall.
>
> Thy gowns, thy shoes, thy beds of roses,
> Thy cap, thy kirtle, and thy posies
> Soon break, soon wither, soon forgotten, –
> In folly ripe, in reason rotten.
>
> Thy belt of straw and ivy buds,
> Thy coral clasps, and amber studs,
> All these in me no means can move
> To come to thee and be thy love.
>
> But could youth last and love still breed,
> Had joys no date nor age no need,
> Then these delights my mind might move
> To live with thee and be thy love.

133 **Letter to André Billy** During the First World War, Apollinaire served in the French artillery and infantry. He survived a skull wound towards the end of the war, but died a few months later in the influenza

epidemic ravaging Paris. In a letter to his friend André Billy, he wrote of his *Calligrammes*: 'They are an idealization of *vers-libre* poetry and of typographical precision at a time when typography is brilliantly ending its career, at the dawn of new methods of reproduction, the cinema and the gramophone.' In the original French text, typography is used to suggest the shape of a bird of prey (as a shell), an eye, and a cathedral (specifically, Notre Dame).

Poème epistolaire

Premier canonnier conducteur
Je suis au front et te salue
Non non tu n'as pas la berlue
Cinquante-neuf est mon secteur

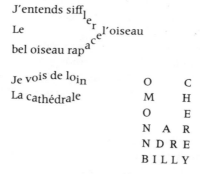

To Emilia V –   Mary Shelley discovered these lines after Shelley's death in one of his notebooks, when she was transcribing his poems for publication. The manuscript draft which we reproduce, the only known source of the poem, was composed at the same time as the opening lines of *Epipsychidion*, Shelley's celebration of love. The same images appear in both texts: music, memory, rose leaves (or petals).

Sweet Spirit! Sister of that orphan one,
Whose empire is the name thou weepest on,
In my heart's temple I suspend to thee
These votive wreaths of withered memory.

Poor captive bird! who, from thy narrow cage,
Pourest such music, that it might assuage
The rugged hearts of those who prisoned thee,
Were they not deaf to all sweet melody;
This song shall be thy rose: its petals pale
Are dead, indeed, my adored Nightingale!
But soft and fragrant is the faded blossom,
And it has no thorn left to wound thy bosom.

(1–12)

Teresa Emilia Viviani, to whom these lines were addressed, was the daughter of the Governor of Pisa. Shelley, who lived in Pisa in 1821–22, visited her in the convent where she was awaiting an arranged marriage, and he took a deep interest in her fate. She wrote sonnets and an essay on Love, a sentence of which Shelley uses as an epigraph to *Epipsychidion* ('Verses addressed to the noble and unfortunate lady, Emilia V –, now imprisoned in the convent of –'). 'Music, when soft voices die' also pays a compliment to Emilia's writing, the 'thoughts' which, when their author is gone, Love itself shall slumber on. Shelley's editors, following Mary Shelley, entitle the lines 'To –,' which we have expanded on the suggestion of the manuscript evidence.

142 **The Lobster Quadrille**   From *Alice in Wonderland*. This poem, which parodies Mary Howitt's ' "Will you walk into my Parlour?" said the spider to the fly', is sung to Alice by the Mock Turtle, while he and his friend the Gryphon 'solemnly' dance on the sea-shore, a moment magically captured by Sir John Gielgud and Malcolm Muggeridge in Jonathan Miller's television version of *Alice*.

144 **I shall say what inordinate love is**   'Inordinate' rather than lawful love is the subject of this lyric. In the original MS, the poem is accompanied by a briefer Latin original (which also appears elsewhere). The Latin treats merely of *Amor* (love), rather than the inordinate variety:

Dicam quid sit Amor: Amor est insania mentis
Ardor inextinctus, insaciata fames
Dulce malum, mala dulcedo, dulcissimus error
Absque labore quies, absque quiete labor.

Of the many English variations on this theme during the Renaissance, probably the most famous is Shakespeare's definition of 'lust' in Sonnet 129:

> Mad in pursuit, and in possession so;
> Had, having, and in quest to have, extreme;
> A bliss in proof, and proved, a very woe,
> Before, a joy proposed; behind, a dream.

45   **A red red Rose**   Burns copied out a slightly different version of this song in a letter to his friend Alexander Cunningham, describing it as 'a simple old Scots song' which he had picked up in the country. Virtually every stanza of the song can be matched in oral tradition and earlier broadsheet ballads, and Burns's editors disagree on the extent to which he may have altered or improved it. But the final version seems unmistakably to have his special touch, in its tenderness and lyricism and its impeccable rhythms.

48   **To Someone Who Insisted I Look Up Someone**   The Editors met the American poet X. J. Kennedy several years ago, and to our surprise he remembered us well. He wrote from Bedford, Massachusetts: 'What a gleeful thing, to have lines perused by London straphangers (or is it pole-clingers?). Your picking that item delighted me more than if the Swedish Academy had handed me the Nobel Prize, and seemed about equally incredible.'

49   **Two Fragments**   Sappho, the great lyric poet of the ancient world, called by Plato 'the Tenth Muse', was born in the late 7th century on the island of Lesbos. Much of her poetry has come to us from fragments of papyrus discovered in the late 19th century; other poems, including the two fragments translated here, were quoted by ancient grammarians.

50   **I Am**   Written in Northampton County Asylum, this is the best known of John Clare's many poems. After a brief period of fame as a 'peasant genius', Clare became more and more disorientated, and lived in mental asylums from 1837 until his death in 1864. The confusion from which he suffered did not affect his lucidity as a poet. He continued until the end to produce work of a high order.

151 **Dream Boogie**   Langston Hughes, born in Joplin, Missouri, was a major figure in the Harlem Renaissance of the 1920s and '30s. 'Dream Boogie' is the first poem of *Montage of a Dream Deferred* (1951), a sequence of poems which use the idiom of bebop to portray the dreams of ordinary men and women in New York's Black ghetto.

155 **The Flaw in Paganism**   Dorothy Parker, poet, journalist and short-story writer, was one of the inner circle of wits and literary celebrities who met regularly for lunch at the Algonquin Hotel in New York in the 1920s. She worked in Hollywood as a scriptwriter, became involved in radical politics, and was blacklisted during the McCarthy period.

   Soon after this poem appeared on the Underground, we received a phone call from a vicar asking permission to reprint it in the *Church Times* – which would have amused the author.

156 **Anthem for Doomed Youth**   'Above all I am not concerned with Poetry. My subject is War, and the pity of War. The Poetry is in the pity' (from Wilfred Owen's draft *Preface* to his war poems). Owen's poetical manifesto has an added poignancy since he was killed in France just seven days before the Armistice. This sonnet contains a bitter parody on the paraphernalia of formal mourning.

158 **A Picture**   Bei Dao ('North Island') is the pen name of Zhao Zhenkai, a leading Chinese dissident writer. He was in Berlin at the time of the Tiananmen Square massacre (4 June 1989), and has been unable since then to return to Beijing, where his wife and daughter live. 'A Picture' was written in 1990, during a six-month stay in Stockholm.

161 **Gray Goose and Gander**   The origins of this charming fragment are unknown. Its first printing is in J. O. Halliwell's *Nursery Rhymes of England*, 3rd Edition (1844).

162 **Sonnet: On His Blindness**   Milton went totally blind in his early forties. In another sonnet on his blindness, written for his friend and pupil Cyriack Skinner, Milton explains that he lost his sight 'In liberty's defence' – that is, through writing his anti-clerical and political pamphlets, including *Areopagitica*, his eloquent plea for freedom of thought and the press.

164   **Late Summer Fires**   The regeneration of the land by setting fire to it is an ancient Aboriginal technique which does not find favour with all modern Australians. Les Murray kindly wrote to us elucidating two phrases in the poem: 'The "hardcourt game" is life in Outback Australia, where soils tend to be pink to ochre to blood red and most often very hard and bare, under the cover of low bush ... So your note could say "hardcourt: refers to the hard red soils of inland Australia." And the Aboriginal flag (black and red, with a yellow disc at the centre), relates to that – the red once again standing for that soil and the blood spilt on it, while the black's for the people and the yellow disc is the sun.'

166   **The Twa Corbies**   First printed in Sir Walter Scott, *Minstrelsy of the Scottish Border* (1802–3). Readers may like to compare the Scots border ballad with the popular English ballad, **The Three Ravens**, first set to music by Thomas Ravenscroft in 1611:

> There were three Ravens sat on a tree,
>> *Downe a downe, hay down, hay downe.*
> There were three Ravens sat on a tree,
>> *With a downe.*
> There were three Ravens sat on a tree,
> They were as blacke as they might be.
>> *With a downe derrie, derrie, derrie, downe, downe.*
>
> The one of them said to his mate,
> Where shall we our breakefast take?
>
> Downe in yonder greene field,
> There lies a Knight slain under his shield.
>
> His hounds they lie downe at his feete,
> So well they can their Master keepe.
>
> His Haukes they flie so eagerly,
> There's no fowle dare him come nie.
>
> Downe there comes a fallow Doe,
> As great with yong as she might goe.
>
> She lift up his bloudy hed,
> And kist his wounds that were so red.
>
> She got him up upon her backe,
> And carried him to earthen lake.

She buried him before the prime,
She was dead her selfe ere even-song time.

God send every gentleman
Such haukes, such hounds, and such a Leman.

167   **The Great Frost**   'Frost fairs' were held on the frozen Thames in the
bitter winters of 1684 and 1698. John Evelyn described the extraordi-
nary scene in his Diary, 24 January 1684: 'Coaches plied from West-
minster to the Temple and from several other stairs to and fro, as in the
streets, sleds, sliding with skates, a bull-baiting, horse and coach races,
puppet plays and interludes, cooks, tippling and other lewd places, so
that it seemed to be a Bacchanalian triumph, or carnival on the water.'

172   **A True and Faithful Inventory**   Printed in *Swift: Poetical Works*,
edited by Herbert Davis (OUP 1967). Thomas Sheridan was an Irish
schoolmaster, one of several friends with whom Swift liked to
exchange puns, riddles and verse epistles.

174   **Thanks Forever**   A modern view of a scene similar to that described
by Walt Whitman in 'Crossing Brooklyn Ferry', in which the poet
stands at the ferry rail imagining later generations standing at the same
spot, gazing at the same river and sky. The first section of Whitman's
poem celebrating his beloved city was displayed on the London Under-
ground, alongside 'Thanks Forever', as part of an exchange of poems
with the New York City Transit Authority:

Flood-tide below me! I see you face to face!
Clouds of the west – sun there half an hour high – I see you
    also face to face.

Crowds of men and women attired in the usual costumes, how
    curious you are to me!
On the ferry boats, the hundreds and hundreds that cross,
    returning home, are more curious to me than you suppose,
And you that shall cross from shore to shore years hence are
    more to me, and more in my meditations, than you might
    suppose . . .

'Let my shadow disappear into yours'   Our contribution to an exchange of poems with Stockholm Transport, which displayed Kipling's 'A Dead Statesman' at the same time, as part of a series of poems by Nobel prizewinners.

from **Requiem**   For seventeen months, the Russian poet Anna Akhmatova queued daily outside the prison in Leningrad where her son was held. This extract from *Requiem* is part of a cycle of poems that covers the years between 1935 and 1940 and commemorates the sufferings of ordinary men and women, victims of Stalin's purges.

The Exiles   From the time of the Highland Clearances until the early years of this century, famine and bitter poverty drove thousands of Highlanders to leave Scotland and emigrate to North America in search of a living. Iain Crichton Smith told us that the starting point for this poem was a visit he made to Canada, when he discovered many familiar Scottish place names.

'My true love hath my heart and I have his'   This famous lyric was first printed in this form by George Puttenham, *The Arte of English Poesie* (1589). Puttenham quotes the poem as an example of 'musicall ditties to be song to the lute or harpe', which suggests that it may have been set to music before 1589. The poem is a shortened version of a sonnet in Book Three of Sidney's *Arcadia*, written for his young sister, Mary, Countess of Pembroke, when Sidney was in his early 20s.

To My Dear and Loving Husband   Anne Bradstreet grew up in the household of the Earl of Lincoln, where her father Thomas Dudley, an ardent Puritan, was steward. In 1630, when she was 18, she emigrated to the Massachusetts Bay Colony with her husband Simon Bradstreet and her father, each of whom later became Governor of the colony. Her poems were published in England in 1650, as *The Tenth Muse Lately Sprung Up in America*. An expanded edition was published in Boston, Massachusetts, in 1678, six years after the poet's death.

Chorus from a Play   From *The Secular Masque*, one of the last works written by Dryden, in which he sums up a century riven by religious war. The reign of Charles I is associated with the huntress Diana:

Then our Age was in its Prime,
Free from Rage, and free from Crime,
A very Merry, Dancing, Drinking,
Laughing, Quaffing, and unthinking Time.

The years of the Civil War belong to Mars:

Set the Martial Mind on Fire,
And kindle Manly Rage.
Mars has lookt the Sky to Red;
And Peace, the lazy Good, is fled.
Plenty, Peace, and Pleasure fly;
    The Sprightly Green
In Woodland-Walks, no more is seen;
The Sprightly Green, has drunk the Tyrian Dye.

The Restoration is the age of Venus:

Calms appear, when Storms are past;
Love will have his Hour at last:
Nature is my kindly Care;
Mars destroys, and I repair;
Take me, take me, while you may,
Venus comes not ev'ry Day.

The final Chorus is addressed by the worldly, disillusioned poet in turn to each presiding deity, first to Diana ('Thy Chase had a Beast in View'); then Mars ('Thy Wars brought nothing about'); lastly Venus: ('Thy lovers were all untrue').

200   **Inversnaid**   Dated September 28, 1881. Burn: a small river or stream. The Snaid burn runs from Loch Arklet to the tiny hamlet of Inversnaid, where it enters Loch Lomond. After seven weeks' service in the Glasgow slums as assistant at St Joseph's Church, Hopkins visited Loch Lomond and spent a few hours at Inversnaid. Several of the unfamiliar terms in the poem are his own coinage.

203   **His Return to London**   Having remained loyal to Charles I, Herrick was ejected in 1647 from his post as vicar at Dean Prior, Devon, and retired to London, where he remained until 1660. Several of Herrick's poems praise the simple pleasures of country life; he is best known as the poet who sings 'of Brooks, of Blossomes, Birds, and Bowers'. But his joy at escaping from Devon to London in 1647 is confirmed by an earlier poem, 'Discontents in Devon':

More discontents I never had
   Since I was born, than here;
Where I have been, and still am sad,
   In this dull Devonshire;
Yet justly too I must confess;
   I ne'er invented such
Ennobled numbers for the Press,
   Than where I loath'd so much.

1–213 **Prizewinners, The TLS/Poems on the Underground Poetry Competition 1996** Our poetry competition on urban themes, sponsored and co-judged by *The Times Literary Supplement*, generated a mass of remarkable material from all parts of the UK and several countries abroad. Entries touched on every aspect of urban life, including praise of a city's history, despair at its decline, cheerful or apocalyptic predictions as to its future. Above all, it was the people of the city who were presented: shopkeepers, city gents, tramps and beggars, a Turkish barber, a Rasta bus-driver, gentle skinheads, transvestites, office cleaners, accountants, children, shoppers. Understandably, many poems were angry, dealing as they did with deprivation and poverty. But others were humane and full of optimism, as they drew attention to the great mix of cultures to be found in any large urban population – especially in London – and to the small pleasures of urban life, the glimpse of a fox, the delights of parks and open spaces and, above all, the river. It was difficult to choose three prizewinning poems out of so many of a high standard, and the ones we chose were not necessarily representative. But we thought each of them offered an original and imaginative glimpse of urban life, and we were delighted to offer them to the public in the final set of the year.

Potosí A silver-mining city in the mountains of Bolivia.

NOTES TO THE POSTERS

After the success of our first collection, *100 Poems on the Underground*, we decided the following year to include a group of full-colour historic London Underground posters, all featuring poetry, in a hardback *Illustrated Edition*. For this much expanded *Anniversary Edition* we have again trawled through the archives at the London Transport Museum, and have selected another 24 posters which appeared on London Underground sites between 1909 and 1958. They all include poetic extracts, ranging from Shakespeare, Milton, Pope and Matthew Arnold, to Swinburne (a great favourite) and Robert Bridges, poet laureate from 1913 to 1930. Sources are identified in our footnotes, below.

following page 32

1 **'Oh, London'**   From the *Induction* to *The Seven Deadly Sins of London* by Thomas Dekker, an 'entertainment' published in 1606. The original passage offers a more rounded picture of the great but sinful city:

> O London, thou art great in glory, and envied for thy
> greatness: thy Towers, thy Temples, and thy Pinnacles
> stand upon thy head like borders of fine gold, thy waters like
> fringes of silver hang at the hemmes of thy garments. Thou
> art the goodliest of thy neighbours, but the proudest; the
> wealthiest but the most wanton. Thou hast all things in thee
> to make thee fairest, and all things in thee to make thee
> foulest; for thou art attir'de like a Bride, drawing all that look
> upon thee, to be in love with thee, but there is much harlot
> in thine eyes.

2 **The Way of Escape to the Countryside**   ('When daisies go, shall winter time')

> When daisies go, shall winter time
> Silver the simple grass with rime;
> Autumnal frosts enchant the pool
> And make the cart-ruts beautiful;
> And when snow-bright the moor expands,
> How shall your children clap their hands!
> To make this earth our hermitage,

A cheerful and a changeful page,
God's bright and intricate device
Of days and seasons doth suffice.

from 'The House Beautiful' by Robert Louis Stevenson,
in *Underwoods* (1887)

3   **The Way of Business**   ('Fleet upon fleet')

> Fleet upon fleet; argosy upon argosy. Masts to the right,
> masts to the left, masts in front, masts yonder above the
> warehouses; masts in among the streets as steeples
> appear amid roofs; masts across the river hung with
> drooping half-furled sails; masts afar down thin and
> attenuated, mere dark straight lines in the distance. They
> await in stillness the rising of the tide.

Richard Jefferies, 'Venice in the East End',
from *The Life of the Fields* (1884)

Jefferies, the great English naturalist, was born and bred in the
Wiltshire countryside. But for a short time, when he was working in
London, he lived at Eltham and entered the town by the South
Eastern railway station at London Bridge. He wrote: 'Nowhere else is
there an entrance to a city like this. Masts are always dreamy to look
at, they speak of a romance of the sea, of unknown lands, of distant
forests aglow with tropical colours and abounding with strange forms
of life. In the hearts of most of us there is always a desire for
something beyond experience.' ('Red Roofs of London', *The Open Air*
[1885]).

4   **Winter's Discontent Made Glorious**   An irreverent misquotation
of the opening lines of Shakespeare's *Richard III*: 'Now is the winter of
our discontent / Made glorious summer by this son of York.'

following page 64

5   **Richmond Park**   ('The Summit of a far-famed Hill') A reference to
Richmond Hill, famous for its views of London and the Thames valley,
and celebrated (under its ancient name of 'Sheen') by the 18th
century poet James Thomson in *The Seasons* (*Summer*, lines 1403ff).
The quotation itself appears to be a conflation of lines by Wordsworth
and Robert Bloomfield (see note 16, below). In Book I of *The Banks of*

Wye, Bloomfield, writing of the hill at Ross-on-Wye and flattering a local patron, makes mention of 'Kyrle's high virtues / Whose own hand clothed this far-famed hill / with reverend elms . . .' Bloomfield was a contemporary of Wordsworth, who, writing in *The Prelude* of his childhood, refers to 'The naked summit of a far-off hill / Beyond the limits that my feet had trod.' That Bloomfield's hill was in Herefordshire and Wordsworth's in Cumberland or Westmorland would not have troubled the gifted, cultured and eccentric team who originally selected these quotations. We have noticed that they were as cavalier with geographical verisimilitude as they were with literary text.

6 **Fancy Dress**   ('Oh worthy fool!') Adapted from Shakespeare, *As You Like It* II.vii.33–34: 'O noble fool! / A worthy fool! – Motley's the only wear.'

7 **In Toyland**   ('Ah, make the most of what we yet may spend') A single line from the most frequently quoted of all Victorian poems, *The Rubaíyát of Omar Khayyám*, translated by Edward Fitzgerald:

> Ah, make the most of what we yet may spend,
> Before we too into the Dust descend;
>> Dust into Dust, and under Dust to lie,
> Sans Wine, sans Song, sans Singer, and – sans End!

8 **At Southend**   ('The Struggle for Existence began on the Seashore') The copywriter has adapted Charles Darwin's explanation for the evolution of man, elucidated in Chapter Three of *The Origin of Species* (1859).

following page 96

9 **Dorking by Motor-Bus**   ('I know these slopes') Adapted from Stanza 12 of *Thyrsis*, Matthew Arnold's elegy for his friend and fellow-poet Arthur Hugh Clough. The full stanza celebrates the countryside near Oxford, and includes Arnold's characteristic lament for the lost innocence of an earlier time:

> I know these slopes; who knows them if not I? –
>> But many a dingle on the loved hillside,
>>> With thorns once studded, old, white-blossomed trees,
>> Where thick the cowslips grew, and far descried

High towered the spikes of purple orchises,
　　Hath since our day put by
The coronals of that forgotten time;
　　Down each green bank hath gone the ploughboy's team,
　　And only in the hidden brookside gleam
Primroses, orphans of the flowery prime.

10　**Wotton Church**　('O sweeter than the marriage-feast') Lines 601–609 from *The Ancient Mariner*, by Coleridge. Nothing to do with Wotton Church, near Dorking; the Ancient Mariner could be telling his compulsive tale of sin and redemption anywhere in the world.

11　**Rambling Parties**　('Away to the green, green country') The sixth stanza of 'Sunday at Hampstead' (*An idle idyll by a very humble member of the great and noble London mob*) by James Thomson ('B.V.'), author of *The City of Dreadful Night*.

12　**'All things above were bright and fair'**　From 'The Slave in the Dismal Swamp', by the American poet Henry Wadsworth Longfellow. This was one of eight poems on slavery published as a pamphlet in 1842, more than twenty years before slavery was abolished in America.

A poor old slave, infirm and lame;
　　Great scars deformed his face;
On his forehead he bore the brand of shame,
And the rags, that hid his mangled frame,
　　Were the livery of disgrace.

All things above were bright and fair,
　　All things were glad and free;
Lithe squirrels darted here and there,
And wild birds filled the echoing air
　　With songs of Liberty!

On him alone was the doom of pain,
　　From the morning of his birth;
On him alone the curse of Cain
Fell, like a flail on the garnered grain,
　　And struck him to the earth!

Though Longfellow was not an active Abolitionist, there could be no doubt where his sympathies lay, and the poems were savagely attacked in the press.

following page 128
Four striking visual images inviting Londoners to explore contrasting natural habitats, all within easy reach of the city by public transport.

13 **River**   ('Search down the marge') From *A Water-Party* by Robert Bridges, and a favourite source for LT copywriters:

> Let us, as by this verdant bank we float,
> Search down the marge to find some shady pool
> Where we may rest awhile and moor our boat,
> And bathe our tired limbs in the waters cool.

14 **Wood**   ('The busy woodpecker') Shelley's love poem, 'To Jane: The Recollection', dated February 22 1822, commemorates a day spent wandering in the pine forest near Pisa, where Shelley was living at the time.

> How calm it was! the silence there
>   By such a chain was bound
> That even the busy woodpecker
>   Made stiller with her sound
> The inviolable quietness;
>   The breath of peace we drew
> With its soft motion made not less
>   The calm that round us grew.

15 **Down**   ('I climb your crown, and lo! a sight surprising') From 'The Downs' by Robert Bridges:

> I climb your crown, and lo! a sight surprising
> Of sea in front uprising, steep and wide:
>   And scattered ships ascending
>   To heaven, lost in the blending
> Of distant blues, where water and sky divide,
> Urging their engines against wind and tide,
>   And all so small and slow
> They seem to be wearily pointing the way they would go.

---

16 **Heath**   ('Then the lone owl awoke from rest') From *The Banks of Wye* by Robert Bloomfield, a farm labourer and shoemaker born near Bury-St-Edmunds in 1766. Bloomfield lived a life of extreme privation, and died in 1823, half blind and in great poverty. The passage quoted refers to the ruined fortress at Chepstow, where,

> E'en on the walls where paced the brave,
> High o'er his crumbling turrets wave
> The rampant seedlings.

following page 160

17 **Windsor Castle**   ('Close by those meads forever crowned with flowers') Pope's lines provide a pleasant excuse for us to quote more extensively from one of the wittiest of all English poets:

> Close by those meads forever crowned with flowers,
> Where Thames with pride surveys his rising towers,
> There stands a structure of majestic frame,
> Which from the neighb'ring Hampton takes its name.
> Here Britain's statesmen oft' the fall foredoom
> Of foreign tyrants, and of nymphs at home;
> Here thou, great ANNA, whom three realms obey,
> Dost sometimes counsel take – and sometimes tea.

> Alexander Pope, *Rape of the Lock*,
> Canto 3, lines 1–8

ANNA: Queen Anne

18, 19   Two complementary images of native grasses and wildflowers, illustrated by Swinburne's sensuous verse.

'Where tides of grass break into foam of flowers'

> Night falls like fire; the heavy lights run low,
> And as they drop, my blood and body so
>   Shake as the flame shakes, full of days and hours
> That sleep not neither weep they as they go.
>
> Ah yet would God this flesh of mine might be
> Where air might wash and long leaves cover me,
>   Where tides of grass break into foam of flowers,
> Or where the wind's feet shine along the sea.

> Algernon Charles Swinburne, from *Laus Veneris*

'Strong blossoms with perfume of manhood', from *Hertha*

> In the spring-coloured hours
>   When my mind was as May's,
> There brake forth of me flowers
>   By centuries of days,
> Strong blossoms with perfume of manhood, shot out from my
>   spirit as rays.
>
>   And the sound of them springing
>   And smell of their shoots
>   Were as warmth and sweet singing
>   And strength to my roots;
> And the lives of my children made perfect with freedom of soul
>   were my fruits.

The speaker is the ancient earth goddess Hertha. Swinburne considered *Hertha* his finest poem.

20 **Hampton Court** ('Rivers are roads which march and / Carry you where you wish to go') A literal translation of Pascal's *Pensées* 717: 'Les rivières sont des chemins qui marchent et qui portent où l'on veut aller.'

following page 192

21 **Out and About by London Transport** ('all your quaint enameld eyes') An extract from Milton's classical elegy for a young Cambridge friend, Edward King, drowned at sea. Milton deliberately chooses English flowers for the 'Sicilian Muse' to strew on the imagined hearse.

> Throw hither all your quaint enameld eyes,
> That on the green terf suck the honied showres,
> And purple all the ground with vernal flowres.
> Bring the rathe Primrose that forsaken dies,
> The tufted Crow-toe, and pale Gessamine,
> The white Pink, and the Pansie freakt with jeat,
> The glowing Violet,
> The Musk-rose, and the well attir'd Woodbine,
> With Cowslips wan that hang the pensive hed,
> And every flower that sad embroidery wears:
> Bid *Amaranthus* all his beauty shed,
> And Daffadillies fill their cups with tears,
> To strew the Laureat Herse where *Lycid* lies.

Lycidas, lines 139–151

22 **Country Walks – Spring**   ('For winter's rains and ruins are over')
The copywriter has taken the first and last lines of a stanza from
Atalanta in Calydon, by Swinburne:

> For winter's rains and ruins are over,
>   And all the season of snows and sins;
> The days dividing lover and lover,
>   The light that loses, the night that wins;
> And time remembered is grief forgotten,
> And frosts are slain and flowers begotten,
> And in green underwood and cover
>   Blossom by blossom the spring begins.

23 **Country Walks – Summer**   ('Where the thistle lifts a purple crown')
The opening lines of 'Daisy', from *Poems on Children* by Francis Thompson.

24 **London Rovers**   ('The height and spread of frontage shining sheer')
It might be interesting to know how many commuters identified the
quotation, which is from *London Voluntaries II* by the Victorian poet
W. E. Henley. The lines describe the 'golden end of afternoon' in
October, as the sunlight transforms ordinary London scenes:

> The windows, with their fleeting, flickering fires,
> The height and spread of frontage shining sheer,
> The quiring signs, the rejoicing roofs and spires –
> 'Tis El Dorado – El Dorado plain,
> The Golden City!

ACKNOWLEDGEMENTS

The editors and publisher gratefully acknowledge permission to reproduce the following copyright poems in this book:

Dannie Abse: 'Mysteries' from *Selected Poems,* © Dannie Abse 1994. Reprinted by permission of Sheil Land Associates.
Fleur Adcock: 'Immigrant' from *Selected Poems* (1983), © Fleur Adcock 1983. Reprinted by permission of Oxford University Press.
Anna Akhmatova: 'Requiem' from *Selected Poems,* translation © Richard McKane 1989. Reprinted by permission of Bloodaxe Books.
Moniza Alvi: 'Arrival 1946' from *The Country at my Shoulder* (1993) © Moniza Alvi 1993. Reprinted by permission of Oxford University Press.
Maya Angelou: 'Come. And Be My Baby' from *Just Give Me A Cool Drink of Water 'Fore I Diiie,* © Maya Angelou 1971. Reprinted by permission of Virago Press.
W. H. Auden: Song ('Stop all the clocks, cut off the telephone') and 'If I could tell you' from *Collected Poems* by W. H. Auden, © W. H. Auden 1968. Reprinted by permission of Faber and Faber.
Bei Dao: 'A Picture' from *Old Snow,* Anvil, © Bei Dao 1990. Reprinted by permission of David Higham Associates.
Gerard Benson: 'The Coming of Grendel' from *Beowulf,* and 'Old English Riddle', © Gerard Benson 1988 and 1990. Reprinted by permission of the author.
Oliver Bernard, translator: 'Letter to André Billy. 9 April 1915' from Guillaume Apollinaire, *Selected Poems* (1986), translation © Oliver Bernard 1986. Reprinted by permission of Anvil Press.
James Berry: 'Benediction' from *Chain of Days* (1985), © James Berry 1985. Reprinted by permission of Oxford University Press.
John Betjeman: 'Summoned by Bells' © John Betjeman 1960. Reprinted by permission of John Murray.
Sujata Bhatt: 'Love in a Bathtub' from *Monkey Fires,* © Sujata Bhatt 1991. Reprinted by permission of Carcanet Press.
Elizabeth Bishop: 'One Art' from *Complete Poems 1927–1979,* © Alice Helen Methfessel 1983. Reprinted by permission of Farrar, Straus and Giroux.
Valerie Bloom: 'Sun a-shine, rain a-fall' from *Duppy Jamboree* (1992) © Cambridge University Press. Reprinted by permission of Cambridge University Press and the author.
Eavan Boland: 'The Emigrant Irish', from *Selected Poems* © Eavan Boland 1986. Reprinted by permission of Carcanet Press.
Edward Kamau Brathwaite: 'Mmenson' from *The Arrivants* (1973), © Edward Kamau Brathwaite 1973. Reprinted by permission of Oxford University Press.
Jean 'Binta' Breeze: 'Moonwise' from *Spring Cleaning,* © Jean 'Binta' Breeze

INDEX OF POETS
AND TRANSLATORS

INDEX OF FIRST LINES

A NOTE OF THANKS

'POEMS ON THE UNDERGROUND' enjoys the cooperation and support of London Transport, which provides advertising spaces free of charge and pays production costs of the programme. We are also grateful for generous financial support from the London Arts Board, the Calouste Gulbenkian Foundation, the Stefan Zweig Programme of the British Library, and the British Council, which displays the Tube posters in its libraries and offices abroad. We owe special thanks to the British Tourist Authority, for sponsoring the Autumn 1995 set of poems as part of the Festival of Arts and Culture, and *The Times Literary Supplement*, for making possible a full display of poems in Autumn 1996, through their sponsorship of The TLS/Poems on the Underground Poetry Competition. We would like also to thank Tom Davidson, who has designed the posters since 1989.

For their invaluable help in the preparation of this *Anniversary Edition*, we join the publishers in thanking Jonathan Riddell of the London Transport Museum and the staff of the LTM archives. We have also received unfailing assistance from the Librarians and staff of the British Library (Manuscripts), the Poetry Library (South Bank Centre), the Northern Poetry Library, and the Richmond Reference Library (Local Studies).

The number of friends and colleagues who have given encouragement and practical advice is too great to list here – to all, our thanks.

Readers may like to know that copies of the Underground poem posters can be purchased from the London Transport Museum. Full details can be obtained by writing to Poems on the Underground, London Transport Museum, Freepost, Covent Garden, London WC2E 7BB. No stamp is required.